Flower of Battle:
MS Latin 11269

Flower of Battle: MS Latin 11269

With Interpretation by
Benjamin Winnick - Translator
Richard Marsden - Interpretation

Formatting – Henry Snider
Cover Art – Henry Snider
Copyright 2018, All Rights Reserved

Without limiting the rights under copyright reserved above, no part of this publication, except images that are public domain or under creative commons, may be reproduced, stored, or introduced into a retrieval system, or transmitted in any form or by any means (electronic, mechanical, photocopying or otherwise) without the prior written permission of both the copyright owner and Tyrant Industries, except in the case of brief quotations embodied in critical reviews.

ISBN 13 978-0-9992903-4-7

Bibliothèque nationale de France

Special thanks to the Bibliothèque nationale de France which allowed Tyrant Industries to purchase the rights to use the images of the Flower of Battle MS Latin 11269. Every image from the manuscript is courtesy of the BnF and is under their copyright. The images cannot be copied or reproduced for commercial purposes without express permission of the BNF.

Special thanks to the J. Paul Getty museum, which has allowed MS Ludwig XV 13 to be copied and used by the public at large through the Getty Open Content program.

INTRODUCTION BY RICHARD MARSDEN

Historical Background

Fiore de Liberi was the son of a knight from Northern Italy who is responsible for some of the oldest Historical European Marital Arts treatises available known as the Flower of Battle. We lack many details about Fiore, but can guess from his introduction and the age of his treatises that he was born around 1340, was active in Northern Italy and died, perhaps in Paris, around 1420.

The Flower of Battle was meant to be a complete system and gifted to Niccolò III d'Este, Marquis of Ferrara, Modena, and Parma. It is unknown if Fiore de Liberi was working in the court of Milan and the book was a gift from one court to another to mark peace, or if Fiore was in the direct employ of the d'Este family.

Much of what we know about Fiore is revealed in the prefaces he wrote. Of himself, he says he desired to learn everything about weaponry and dedicated his life to the use of arms.

> *I learned these skills from many German and Italian masters and their senior students, in many provinces and many cities, and at great personal cost and expense. And by the grace of God I also acquired so much knowledge at the courts of noblemen, princes, dukes, marquises, counts, knights and squires, that increasingly I was myself asked to teach. My services were requested many times by noblemen, knights and their squires, who wanted me to teach them the art of armed combat both for fighting at the barrier and for mortal combat. And so I taught this art to many Italians and Germans and other noblemen who were obliged to fight at the barrier, as well as to numerous noblemen who did not actually compete.*[1]

The world he lived in was one rife with conflict. The Holy Roman Empire was Germanic in nature, yet claimed Italy as theirs. The Emperor held only nominal power over his vast territory which was made up of hundreds of kingdoms, duchies, Bishoprics, free-cities and so on.

Italy meanwhile was just as divided amongst competing city-states, feudal kingdoms, and the Papacy which had its own territory, but was missing a Pope who was ensconced in Avignon, France. Those wishing the Papacy to rule Italy, known as the Guelphs fought viciously against the Ghibellines who preferred the nobility to rule with the blessing of the Holy Roman Empire. These factions could be found anywhere in Italy before, during and well-after Fiore's lifetime. Machiavelli, who was born roughly half a century after Fiore's death, complained about such factionalism. Florence could hardly unite when its own populace was riddled with factionalism. Florence's experiences were not unusual in Italy.

During Fiore's formative years Italy was flooded with foreign mercenaries who had trekked over the Alps in the 1361 after there was a pause in the Hundred Years War. John Hawkwood, for example, was a famous English mercenary active in Italy from 1361 to his death in 1394. During his colorful career he worked for numerous Italian city-states. Fiore would have been in his prime at the same time and exposed to martial men from England, France, the Holy Roman Empire and of course Italy.

Italians were already experienced in mercenary warfare before the influx of foreign mercenaries in 1361. Condottiere was the term used to describe mercenaries in Italy, deriving from the word contract. These mercenaries signed contracts with their employers and acted not only as a city-state's army, but could also do garrison duty and any other martial task that the citizenry would rather avoid. Italian rulers were also known to sell their services. Niccolò III d'Este, to whom the Flower of Battle was dedicated, was also a famous condottieri. Fiore also took up arms for money. In 1384 the nobles of

---

Translation by Colin Hatcher

the city of Udine hired Fiore to raise and train soldiers to fight against a Cardinal in the never-ending Guelph and Ghibelline struggle. Afterward, Fiore was given the task of maintaining the peace, acting as a sort of policeman for the city. When peace was arranged, Fiore vanished from the records, likely leaving the city and looking for work yet again.

The business of teaching martial arts in Fiore's lifetime was plagued with, in his opinion, by poor masters. He fought five duels, wearing no armor, against such masters. His students, of which he names several, were all men of note, including condottieri. Fiore indicates in his preface that when teaching his techniques, he taught privately, or with only the student's family as witnesses. Fillipo Vadi called Fiore's art one that was secret and the art of princes and kings.[2]

While Fiore did raise mercenary soldiers and train them, when he trained individuals it was for a different purpose. Mercenaries needed to know how to march and drill and stay in formation during combat as well as follow orders and signals. The Flower of Battle is different in its intent. It teaches one on one combat in a variety of settings tailored to Fiore's noble audience. Fiore discusses the public duel, or what he calls fighting in the barriers. Nobles could fight one another over matters of honor in a public setting. These were not judicial duels, but had similar elements. There were wooden barriers to contain the fight, a stand for an audience to watch and an overseeing lord who could start and end the fight. The fights were generally not fatal on the account of the armor being worn.

One of Fiore's students, Galeazzo fought two duels against the French knight Boucicaut over a matter of honor. At first, attempts were made to prevent the duel from happening, which was customary. However, twelve-thousand people had arrived for their first encounter and they surely expected a fight!

> *...the Lord of Padua and the Lord of Mantua tried to see to it that the combatants would reconcile, but to no avail. Those attempting this with Boucicaut and with Galeazzo went now to one, now to the other combatant for two hours without affecting anything— measuring spears, axes and other armament. Upon seeing that no agreement could be reached, Mr. Boucicaut decided not to wait any longer, had his horse brought to him and mounted it, wearing his helmet, carrying his target before his chest and a spear in his hand. He began pacing around the field, waiting for Galeazzo to also mount his horse. Galeazzo took his horse by the reins and waited for the gauntlet of combat to be thrown.*
>
> *Galeazzo took his horse by the reins and waited for the gauntlet of combat to be thrown. Seeing that Galeazzo would not get on his horse, however, Boucicaut dismounted, headed for his chair and had his spurs removed (it had been agreed that if one of them were to go to his chair, the other should not give himself any trouble). His spurs removed, Mr. Boucicaut grabbed his spear and boldly proceeded against Mr. Galeazzo, thinking that the gauntlet had already been thrown.[3]*

The tossing of the gauntlet remained a mainstay in dueling culture up until the 17th century when a glove might be sent to an opponent.

> *Now, Mr. Michael of Rabara did throw the gauntlet of combat. When they saw this, Mr. Galeazzo and Mr. Boucicaut boldly went against one another on foot with spears. Mr. Galeazzo had his helmet visor raised, and as he saw that Boucicaut was coming towards him also in that same condition, spear-in-hand[4] he hit Boucicaut's aventail in such a way that the latter recoiled by three steps. Mr. Boucicaut threw away his spear and put his hands on Galeazzo's, broke it and reached for his axe which was nearby.*
>
> *He brandished it with both hands and headed for Galeazzo, but the Lord of Mantua, along with the Lord's regulars, ran towards him and grabbed him by the waist saying:*

---

2   While it is clear Fillipo Vadi used Fiore's work as a model for his own, he does not mention Fiore by name. He does however use his language and imagery.

3   Account provided by Greg Mele and translation by Tom Leoni.

4   The wording, *con la sua lanza in mano* suggests that the blow was delivered without letting the spear run through the forward hand.

> *"No more! You have already done much, now do you not want to honor what you have promised and sworn on the missal—to do the wishes of the Lord of Padua and me?"*
>
> *On the other side, the Lord of Padua with his regulars had gone to Mr. Galeazzo and after grabbing him in the same way and saying the same words that were said to Mr. Boucicaut, he eventually reconciled them after much talking.*

Thus the duel ended with neither party being very-much hurt. The two would meet again in another duel and once again, neither was much hurt for it. Fiore gives clues as to the nature of armored combat stating he would much prefer it to fighting without armor. With armor, one could miss a cover and still survive while without one missed cover could be fatal.

Fiore's students were not amateurs in the arts of war. They were military men and as such, Fiore's Flower of Battle has the assumption that whoever is reading it has the basic understanding of martial arts. Little time is spent on how to move or where to cut and thrust, and none at all on how to hold a sword. Instead, the Flower of Battle teaches by example and shows settings that would be plausible in a duel, such as the type fought between Boucicaut and Fiore's student Galeazzo, as well as self-defense. In one example, a man seated with a baton, a symbol of military office, is attacked by a dagger-wielding opponent. No duel is this! Fiore also depicts a man with a walking stick and dagger being set upon by another wielding a spear, another example that is outside of the barriers. Fiore's art also details less than honorable techniques, such as loading blinding powder in the head of a poleaxe. He also shows on horseback how a man with a spear set against a man with a sword can simply stab his unfortunate opponent's horse in the eye.

History of the Four Copies of the Flower of Battle

Today, four copies of his Flower of Battle survive.

MS Ludwig XV 13 is known as the Getty because it is kept in the Getty museum in California.

MS M.383 is known as the Morgan because it is kept in the Morgan museum in New York.

MS Pisani Dossi is known as the Novati. A facsimile was made in the early 20th century by Francesco Novati and the original is kept in the family vaults of the Pisani Dossi family.

MS Latin 11269 has a variety of names including, *Florius de Arte Luctandim*, the Latin and finally, the Paris because the treatise is kept at the Bibliothèque nationale de France.

This book explores the youngest of the surviving treatises, the Paris. The Paris is perhaps the most unusual copy of the Flower of Battle. It was discovered in 2008 by Ken Mondschien and unlike the other copies, is in full-color with hand painted images. The people are drawn with and without armor, or a mixture of both, which fits well with Fiore's approach, a system that could work in or out of armor.

The accuracy of the treaty is questionable. Jay Lecese, an art historian, noted trends throughout the four manuscripts. Looking closely at artist choices, Lecese was able to see a trend that indicated the Getty is likely the original, the Morgan a copy of that and the Novati/Pisani Dossi are copies of the Morgan. Examples of evidence for this can be seen in how an artistic choice, such as perspective is modified from the Getty to the Morgan and then again in the Paris. Lecese's opinion is that he cannot be a hundred percent sure that his theory is correct, but the artistic evidence is strongly suggestive.

The rediscovery of the Paris version was a matter of happenstance. Ken Mondschien was in France and decided on a whim to investigate the Bibliothèque nationale to see if there were any historical European martial arts treatises that were not commonly known. Ken was taken to a large reading room with tall shelves and dusty books that had not been looked at in over a century. There were no modern records as to what manuscripts were even available and so he looked over an early 20th century catalogue. With nothing to go on, he looked at a list of names and noted down any that might be a potential lead.

There, amongst many other titles, he noted a treatise titled *Florius de Arte Luctandi*. Not expecting much, Ken asked to see the treatise in question, but the library's policy was that microfilm had to be examined first before the actual manuscript would be presented. Dutifully, Ken looked the microfilm over and noted an inconsistency. The text he saw was quite clearly Greek and had not titled Florius. He asked to see the actual manuscript and waited, still not expecting to discovery anything groundbreaking.

What Ken was presented with was a lost copy of Fiore's Flower of Battle. Many questions arose; chief among them was, how did a copy of Fiore's work ended up in Paris? Digging in, Ken discovered that the Florius had been purchased centuries ago and taken to France. There, it languished, hardly noticed and improperly documented on microfilm.

While wanting to go immediately to the public, he remained quiet on the discovery to better validate what it was.

Unlike the other treatises, the Paris does not have an introduction, or if it did, it is missing. The treatise was created around 1420, but the cover and title page is from the 17th century indicating a rebinding. There are also questions about why the book is ordered the way it is and it appears as if some of the pages are out of order, at least when compared to the more complete Getty.

The entirety of the Paris is written in Latin. During the 15th century Latin was not just the domain of priests, but was fast-becoming the language of the educated and a hallmark of humanism. While there was profound interest in Latin and the works of the ancients, such as that of Cicero, the understanding of Latin was not the same as it had been. The Church had been using Latin since the fall of the Roman Empire, but had modified it over time to suit their needs creating what is known as Medieval Latin. Humanists of the 15th century wanted to go back to the sources and use Latin in its purest form. This could be as simple as using traditional language structure or as extreme as using only words that exist within Cicero's speeches, an idea Erasmus found foolish. The end result was a new form of Latin called Renaissance Latin that tried to mimic the original. The Paris copy of the Flower of Battle is written, not in ecclesiastical Latin, but in what would have been at the time, the new and exciting Renaissance Latin.

Translating the Latin is thus fraught with difficulties. There was no standardization of just exactly how to write in Renaissance Latin in the early 15th century. The translator, Benjamin Winnick noted that, different words could be used to mean the same thing and his introduction delves further into the intricacies of the language and challenges of translating the Paris.

How Fiore Organized his Work

Throughout the Flower of battle Fiore depicts types of combat that are organized visually and contain text to further explain what is taking place. The sections are, wrestling, fighting with the dagger, the sword in one hand, the sword in two, the spear, the pole-axe, odds and ends and mounted combat. His purpose for writing was to be remembered for his art, yet secrecy still remained. Fiore's works were created before the printing-press, and as such, each surviving manuscript is a work of art that is an expensive endeavor. Some of the treatises have actual gold or silver pressed into the vellum pages! So, while Fiore did write a book it was not meant for the general public, or as Vadi put it, it was the secret art of princes and kings.

Fiore de Liberi explains in the Getty, Morgan and Pisani Dossi how he organized his works. He uses visual cues to tell the readers who is doing what and why. The Paris copy does not always follow this structure in what appears to be artistic mistakes when comparing the Paris to the others. Furthermore, the Paris lacks much of the detail and instruction due to a lack of preface and other informative parts. Below, the general organization and terms of Fiore are provided based off the three other manuscripts.

Master = In Fiore's work, anyone with a crown on their head is a master. There are three types of masters. The first is in a guard (that is usually named), awaiting an attack and is called the First Master of Battle. The other is performing a technique, called a play, and he is called the Remedy Master or Second Master of Battle. The last is a Counter-Master who defeats a play and is called the Third Master of Battle. The Third Master of Battle wears a crown, but also a golden garter under the knee. In the Interpretation those wearing crowns are simply called Masters and those with crowns and garters are called Counter-Masters. When clarity is needed, or there is a discrepancy between the Paris and other manuscripts, it is noted.

This Master is in the Long guard. He is a First Master of Battle.

This Master is starting a series of plays. He is the Second Master of Battle or Remedy Master.

This Master is countering a play. He is the Third Master of Battle or Counter-Master.

Student = Remedy Masters show a play and afterward there are additional plays. Those follow up plays are conducted by the Student. The Student wears a golden garter under his knee. In the interpretation he is called a Student.

The Student is performing a play after a Remedy

Player = The person attacking the Master and being defeated by him and his Students is called the Player and has no markings at all, meaning no crown or garter. In the interpretation he is referenced as the Opponent.

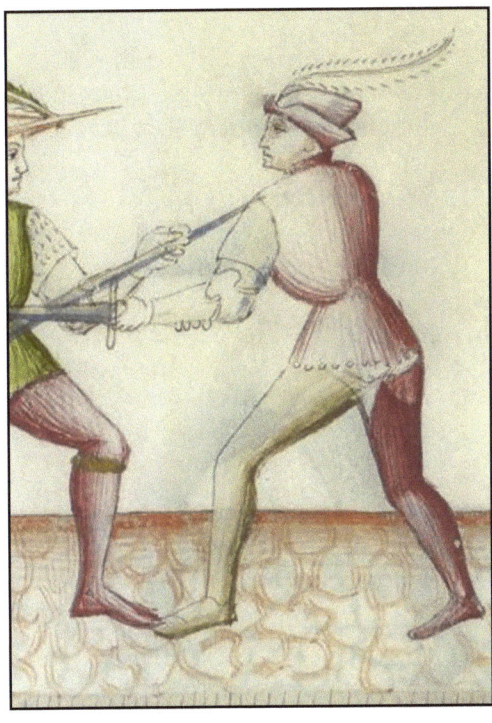

The Player is being defeated either by a Remedy Master or a Student.

A typical outline is to show various First Masters in named guards. Then Fiore shows a Second Master, sometimes called Remedy Master, performing a play against a Player. Then Fiore shows a variety of Students performing variations of the play against various Players. Finally, a Third Master, or Counter-Master is shown defeating the play of a Student. Thus, a guard leads to a remedy, a remedy to a variety of plays, and these plays can be defeated by a counter.

There are exceptions throughout the manuscripts, such as Students following up on the action of prior Students and not the Master, or what appears to be a First Master in a guard, yet no guard is named. There are also, rarely, counters to the Third Master, but Fiore is clear that such actions are difficult and dangerous. To make matters even more complicated, the Paris has numerous Counter-Masters who are likely Masters, and some images appear out of order when compared to the other treatises.

Fiore in the Getty and Morgan routinely has Students refer to other plays from other sections. Meaning, in the sword in one hand section, there are references to the dagger section and in the pole-axe section there are references to the sword in two hand section and so forth. The Paris does not have such direct references. However, Fiore's work should be seen as a system using numerous weapons. Even though Fiore may not explicitly say, a technique from wrestling can be used in the plays of the axe, it is always good to try and assume that this can be done.

The order of sections is different between the surviving copies. The Paris follows the framework of the Morgan starting with mounted, then spear vs mounted, spear, poleaxe, sword in one hand, sword in two hands, armored fencing, sword vs dagger, dagger, and grappling.

How exactly to cut and thrust is not discussed in any of the manuscripts, but where to cut and thrust is. Fiore divides up cuts into broad categories. A *fendente* is a cut that is angled from the opponent's teeth to their knee. It can be done on the right or left side. A *sottani* is its opposite, a cut from the knee to the forehead along the same lines. Between the *fendetne* and *sottani* are the *mezzani*, cuts that are between the knee and forehead, and on the left side is always done with the false edge. Thrusts are divided into upper and lower and left and right.

Fiore discusses footwork only briefly to define his terms which are used throughout the manuscripts.

The footwork includes; an advance of the lead foot to move closer to the opponent, a pass, in which the rear foot becomes the lead and a pass back, in which the lead foot becomes the rear. Stationary rotations include shifting the weight and stance from one leg to the other leading to back-weighted guards. In one play, the Villain's Blow, Fiore specifically suggests to stand with the feet closer together, indicating that in most other plays he prefers them farther apart.

A common use of footwork is when the front foot advances, a little, and moves off the line. The line is an imaginary line connecting the two fighters. After the front foot advances off the line, (it is debatable at to which direction), the rear foot passes at an angle. The direction of the rear foot is easier to figure out because the pass has only one option to travel.

When it comes to measure, it is mentioned in the sword in two hand section that there are two types, *zogho largo*, the wide plays and *zogo stretto*, the narrow plays. In the wide play, the left leg is leading, though there is debate if this is always necessary. In the narrow play the right leg is always leading, so that the off-hand can easily perform offensive actions.

A depiction of animals is used to express traits. These animals represent the four cardinal virtues of fencing according to Fiore. The Paris does depict the animals in what is called a *segno*. They are the lynx, the tiger, the lion and the elephant.

Interpretation

While the Paris can stand on its own as a work of art and a window into the past, it struggles to inform its readers as to how the system works. The Latin gives only snippets of information and no clear directions.

To better understand the translations, I have provided my own interpretations which are derived from comparing the Paris to the other copies of the Flower of Battle. At times I have made direct references and included art from the Getty to help clarify the Paris.

I was assisted by my own club, the Phoenix Society of Historical Swordsmanship as well as Colin Hatcher and Tracy Mellow who gave insight and critique as well as suggestions to make the Paris' interpretation in-line with the Getty translation Colin completed earlier.

The Paris' strength is in its beautiful, full-color artwork, and sense of perspective. Its' weakness is in the limited nature of the Latin text. My hope is that my humble efforts can improve upon the treatise's textual weakness without taking away from its visual strength.

The image on the left is from the Paris, which shows a crowned Master. However, the instructions and art from the Getty, shown on the right, indicate that this is a Counter-Master. The Getty describes how if the attackers' spear is pushed to the right, he can pass forward and rotate his spear so as to strike the opponent in the face with the metal capped end. The Paris, meanwhile, shows the head of the spear being used. Both the lack of a garter and the use of the spear's tip are likely errors in the Paris.

The interpretation will attempt to not only explain the Paris, but also call out what are likely errors in the creation or order of the material when compared to the more complete and easier to understand Getty.

INTRODUCTION BY BENJAMIN WINNICK

When I walked into my first HEMA session with Richard Marsden and the Phoenix Society of Historical Swordsmanship, I did not imagine that it would give me the opportunity to publish a translation of such a fascinating text. This martial arts club was also a hub of scholarship and discovery and as a teacher of the Latin language, my skills were in demand. Although I am relatively inexperienced in HEMA, I happened to be in the right place at the right time.

The first thing that stands out about, the Paris, or *Florius de Arte Luctandi* or *MS Latin 11269* is the beauty of its artwork. None of the other three surviving copies of this text have so much color and such intricate designs throughout the text. The manuscript begins with an elaborate diagram describing the four characteristics of a swordsman, each of which is represented by an animal. A lynx represents caution or *prudentia*, a tiger represents speed or *celeritas*, a lion represents daring or *audacia*, and an elephant represents strength or *fortitudo*. Some practitioners of HEMA take this diagram very seriously and regard one of these animals as a personal totem. I remember having a lively post-tournament discussion with some HEMA practitioners about which animal best represents each of us. This diagram also lists the nine guards with a rough approximation of where to position the sword for each of these guards.

After that it's straight into business. Each page contains two drawings with one or two, or occasionally three or four, paragraphs describing the actions they portray. Unlike the other known copies of Fiore de'i Liberi's manual, this manuscript seems to skip around in its topics and does not proceed from simplest to most complicated. The manuscript starts with horseman v. horseman (2R-5V), moves onto footman v. horsemen (6R-6V), then describes spear v. spear (6V-8R), clubs v. spear (8R), club and dagger v. spear (8V), three-pronged spear (*tricuspis*) v. three-pronged spear (*tricuspis*) (8V-9V), unarmed v. three-pronged spear (*tricuspis*) (10R), one-handed sword v. one-handed sword (10R-12R), two-handed longsword v. two-handed longsword (12V-19V), dagger v. two-handed longsword (20R-20V), unarmed v. dagger (21R-23V), unarmed wrestling (24R), more unarmed v. dagger (24R-25V), more longsword v. longsword (26R-30V), more unarmed v. dagger (31R-34V), more wrestling (35R), more unarmed v. dagger (35R-36R), dagger v. dagger (36V-37R), dagger v. unarmed (this time the dagger-wielder wins) (37V-38R), more wrestling (38V-42V), unarmed v. dagger (unarmed wins) (43R), and finally more dagger v. unarmed (dagger-wielder wins) (43R-44R). It is unclear why the sections are interspersed like this.

The use of the first and second person in the text breathes life into the actions portrayed. The winner is always an 'I' and the loser is always a 'you.' The combatants are speaking to us as they throw us to the ground and impale us with their overwhelming skill. When there are multiple possibilities, our instructor threatens "I will do many bad things to you." Instead of observing from a detached, third-person perspective, we the reader are thrown headlong into the melee where our instructors proudly display their mastery.

The text itself is written, somewhat clumsily, in dactylic hexameter. This was a form of Latin and Greek verse that was mostly used in epic poetry. However, it could be used in other types of poetry as well and became the most standard and recognizable Latin meter, like iambic pentameter in English verse. Yet while English verse relies on patterns of stressed and unstressed syllables, Latin verse used patterns of long and short syllables. Classical Latin verse had strict rules about what made a syllable long or short. The author of this text occasionally played loose with those rules but there is no mistaking that this text was written in dactylic-hexameter. To keep the meter, the author also swapped certain words with their synonyms, which explains many inconsistencies in word-choice.

The manuscript shows signs of use, including tiny annotations and alternate translations written on top of words. Whoever owned this text must have worked hard to understand it. Read the footnotes for individual instances of these annotations and what they might mean.

I want to thank Charlélie Berthaut, whose transcription of the text was immensely helpful to me. The medieval script, in which letters are stacked on top of each other as often as they are placed side-to-side, would have been indecipherable to me and the text's annotations would have escaped my notice without Berthaut laying the groundwork. His French translation of the text provided a great point of reference for me as well.[5]

I would also like to thank Dr. David Christenson, my former professor and graduate advisor. This was my first attempt at a professional translation and Dr. Christenson's guidance on medieval manuscript traditions and paleography was invaluable.

I would also like to thank my friend and former classmate Jesse Muñoz M.A. for help with some of the trickier bits of metrical scansion. Jesse's understanding of Latin verse is unmatched and he was a valuable resource.

And of course, I must thank Richard Marsden, my co-author and HEMA instructor. Over the past two years, his lessons have provided and endless supply of thrills, chills, and spills. Although one of the world's greatest practitioners of Historic European Martial Arts, Richard is always available to teach novices like myself and give in-depth personal guidance. It was his idea to write this book and it has been a tremendous opportunity for me.

---

[5] Any errors or deficiencies in the translation or commentary are the responsibility of the authors.

INTRODUCTION BY HENRY SNIDER

My restorative/recreation work on images and their presentation has kept me serving the legal system for over two decades, enhancing, restoring, and presenting said images in both civil and criminal courts as a media specialist with an emphasis on 3-D accident reconstruction.

I met Richard Marsden through our joint passion for writing, and served early-on serving as a layout artist for fiction works. When he discovered my abilities to clean/ create such works and covers as his *Polish Saber* (©2015), *Historical European Martial Arts - In Its Context* (©2016), and *The Flower of Battle - MS Ludwig XV 13* (©2017), our relationship solidified into what it is today. As with the first time I worked with him, I find Richard a quick-witted fount of knowledge that always keeps me on my toes.

The pages within this book served as a larger challenge because of mirrored page bleed over due to the age of the works and improper care. I found myself not only removing the existing text of each page to make room for the translation, but cleaning the ghost images left on many of the pages. My goal throughout has been to leave as many of the non-destructive imperfections (water and age stains, tears, etc.) to keep as much as the original "feel" as possible.

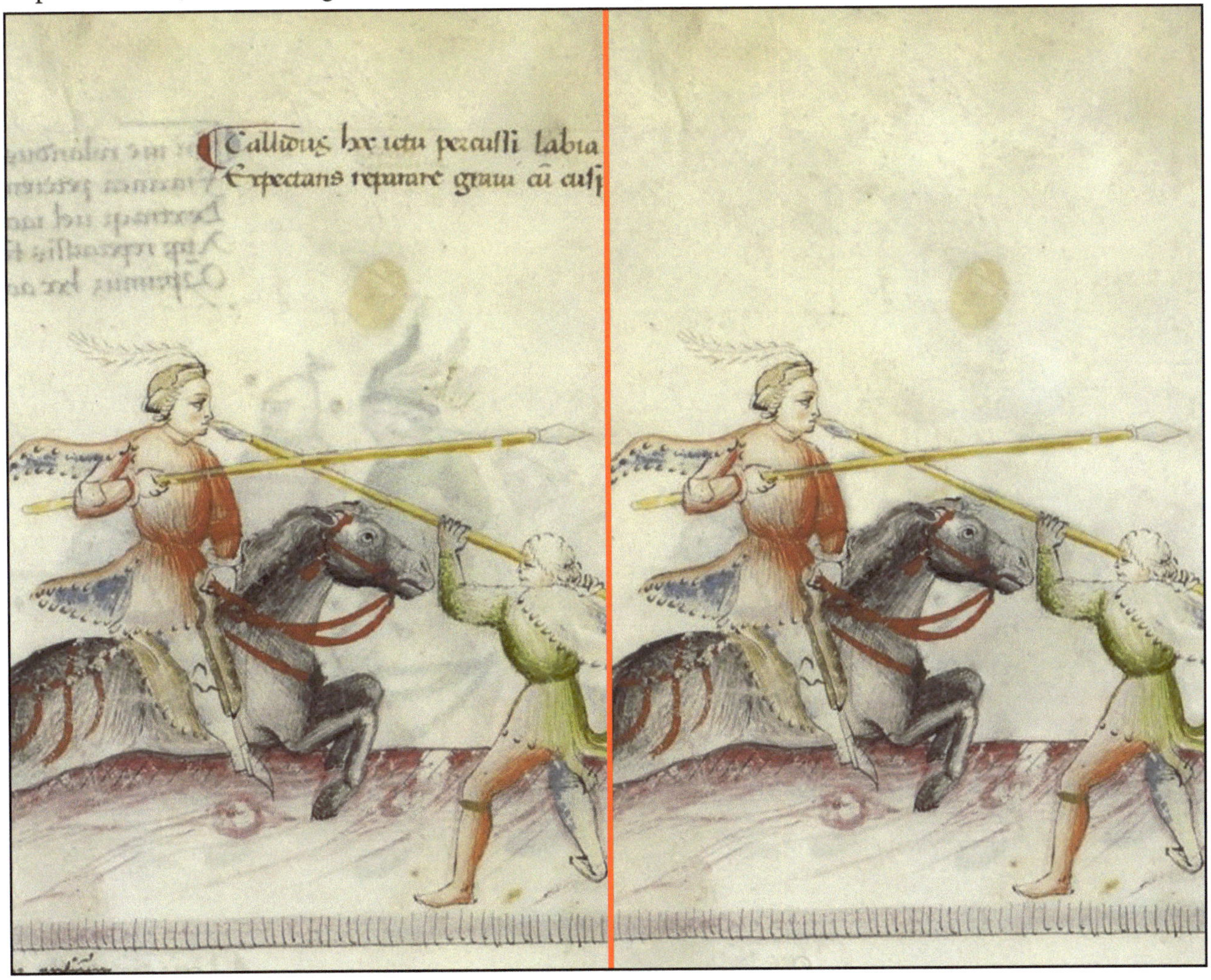

Original and restored image 6v.

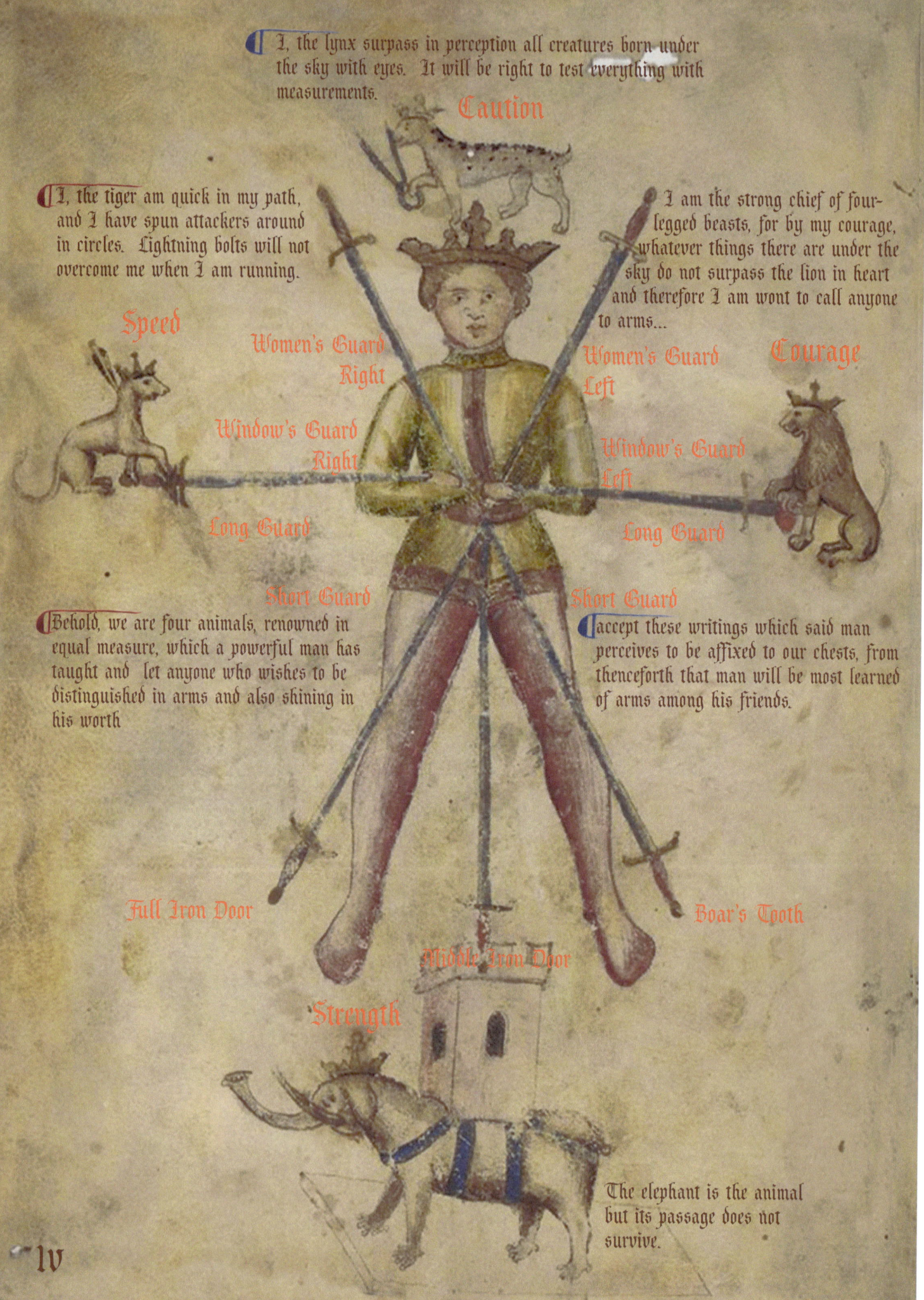

Florius de Arte Luctandi (MS Latin 11269)
Translation by Benjamin Winnick

1v:

Introduction: *Behold, we are four animals, renowned in equal measure, which a powerful man has taught and[1] let anyone who wishes to be distinguished in arms and also shining in his worth accept these writings which said man perceives to be affixed to our chests, from thenceforth that man will be most learned of arms among his friends.*

Caution: *I, the lynx surpass in perception all creatures born under the sky with eyes. It will be right to test everything with measurements.*

The head is marked by a lynx holding dividers, signifying distance. The lynx represents the virtue of Prudence. A fighter needs to know his measure and that of his opponent.

Speed: *I, the tiger am quick in my path, and I have spun attackers[2] around in circles. Lightning bolts will not overcome[3] me when I am running.*

The right hand, and in reference to arms in general, is the tiger holding an arrow, signifying speed. The tiger represents the virtue of Celerity. The hands must be fast, to strike or cover with any weapon. In term of mythology, the Tiger was known in Fiore's day to be a creature of unbelievable speed.

Courage: *I am the strong chief of four-legged beasts, for by my courage, whatever things there are under the sky do not surpass the lion in heart and therefore I am wont to call anyone to arms...*

The left side is marked by the lion holding a heart, signifying courage. The lion represents the virtue of Audacity. A fighter must have the courage to face mortal combat without fear.

Strength: **The elephant is the animal but its passage does not survive.**

The feet are marked by the elephant with a tower on its back, signifying stability. The elephant represents the virtue of Fortitude. The feet must be stable, supported by strength. Wide and stable stances are common throughout Fiore's system. In terms of mythology it was believed elephants were strong creatures, but lacked knees and once brought to the ground could not get up again.

AROUND THE MASTER WRITTEN IN RED FROM TOP-LEFT CLOCKWISE:
Women's' guard right, Women's' guard left, Windows' guard right, Windows' guard left, Long guard, Short guard, Full iron door, Middle iron door, Boar's tooth

---

1   The word is hard to make out. Charlelie Berthaut just labels it as '?ot' and explains "peut-être un nombre (7, 4,), peut-être indéclinable (cf. « ot » final), qui irait avec « potens quisque »," (maybe a number (7, 4), maybe indeclinable (cf. « ot » ending), that would go with « potens quisque »,"). To me, the word appears to be 'et' (and). This also makes sense because it appears to precede another clause.
2   Subitos: literally 'sudden men.'
3   Superabunt: literally 'will conquer.'

2r Top

(Text missing) I bear on pushing (with horns)[4] under the boar's tooth, and in order that I may be able to change many things I will pierce your innards.

The crowned master is in the guard of Boar's Tooth with a shorter lance than that of his opponent. As the opponent charges, the master will bring his lance up and to the right, beating aside the opponent's lance. The master's lance will strike the opponent in the body, while the opponent's will miss.

2r Bottom

Behold, I come holding back my lance to my chest in the woman's position. I do not fear to touch the ground with my slow knees and I will strike varied blows nevertheless, your lance perishes.

The crowned master is carrying his shorter lance in the Woman's Guard on the left. While the prior play had the lance come from below to deflect the incoming attack, this play has the master ready to deflect the blow from above. As before, the incoming attack is beaten to the master's right and he will strike his opponent while his opponent will miss.

---

4 Coruscans: thrusting with horns.

(Text missing) I bear on pushing (with horns) under the boar's tooth, and in order that I may be able to change many things I will pierce your innards.

Behold, I come holding back my lance to my chest in the woman's position. I do not fear to touch the ground with my slow knees and I will strike varied blows nevertheless, your lance perishes.

¶ The regal woman's position is fitting and by striking you with the blade and by charging against you this soul will pass over to the shadows. May the spirits of heaven favor him in some way.

¶ Holding my limbs together I fiercely grip my spear in the middle, you will have been delayed to break it, in the end your horse will go down when it is struck with a lethal wound.

2v

2v Top

The regal woman's position is fitting and by striking you with the blade[5] and by charging[6] against you this soul will pass over to the shadows. May the spirits of heaven favor him in some way.

The crowned master is in the Woman's Guard on the left. When riding to the right side of the opponent, the master will beats his opponent's attack to the right. This is noted in the Morgan and Getty as effective against all weapons.

2v Bottom

Holding my limbs together I fiercely grip my spear in the middle, you will have been delayed to break it, in the end your horse[7] will go down when it is struck with a lethal wound.

The man on the left is shown wearing the crown of the master, however, the instructions in the Getty and Morgan indicate the man on the right should be wearing it. The man on the right with the sword is in the Boar's Tooth guard. As the lancer attacks, the man will deflect the attack to the right, using the false edge of sword. Immediately after, he will bring his sword around and strike his opponent.

From the Getty MS Ludwig XV 13.

---

5 Above this word (*mucrone*) is written 'de la pointe': from the point (*in French*). The owner annotated this manuscript liberally to facilitate his understanding of the text. While most of his annotations are in Latin, this one is in French. Many of the following footnotes discuss these annotations.

6 Furens: literally 'raging'

7 Two words for horse are given: 'Sonipes' and above that 'equus.' Since 'equus' was written above 'sonipes' and appears to have been erased or faded, it seems to be the manuscript owner's addition.

3r Top

Standing up into the opposite side I will perhaps make pains for you, I who while fleeing am unable to defend my own body.

The crowned master is shown wearing armor and has a horse wearing protective material as well. However, in the Getty and Morgan it is noted that the master is unarmored on a horse built for speed and being chased. While fleeing, the master delivers thrusts over his shoulder and behind at his chasing opponent. The master could turn his horse to the right and enter into the Boar's Tooth or Woman's Guard on the left and perform the prior plays.

3r Bottom

This fourth method of bearing does not of course move the blade to the plays, and I will strike you straight away with the sharp point[8] and the hewing will cut your exposed limbs. And again you will clearly leave your seat having lost your sword and this movement has rarely failed a man.

The crowned master is in the guard of the Long Tail. From here, if he rides to his opponent's right side he can beat aside attacks with the true edge of his sword. The Getty and Morgan both warn to deflect attacks horizontally and to the right, not vertically.

---

[8] There is an illegible annotation above 'acuta cuspide' (*with the sharp point*).

¶ Standing up into the opposite side I will perhaps make pains for you, I who while fleeing am unable to defend my own body.

¶ This fourth method of bearing does not of course move the blade to the plays, and I will strike you straight away with the sharp point and the hewing will cut your exposed limbs. And again you will clearly leave your seat having lost your sword and this movement has rarely failed a man.

¶ With the point of the blade I pierce through the exposed throat for the third master taught me with his doctrine.

¶ I terrify the neck with a wound while struggling against a wound. Indeed a prior master secure in his sword teaches this to me.

3v:

3v Top

> With the point of the blade I pierce through the exposed throat for the third master taught me with his doctrine.[9]

The crowned master was in the Long Tail guard and while passing to the right of his opponent he has deflected the opponent's attack horizontally. The master's blade has struck his opponent in the face with a thrust, but he could also choose to thrust at the neck or body.

3v Bottom

> I terrify the neck with a wound while struggling against a wound. Indeed a prior master secure[10] in his sword teaches this to me.

The crowned master is depicted as a student in the other treatises. Having deflected an attack from the Long Tail guard, the master has chosen to strike his opponent in the head with a cut instead of a thrust. This would be done if the opponent's head was unarmored.

The master in the Long Tail guard.

---

9   The word is 'lege.' Although the primary translation is 'law,' it can be translated many ways. Doctrine seems like the most sensible choice.
10   The word is 'cautus,' the perfect passive participle of the semi-deponent caveo, cavere: to be careful, to be on one's guard. Berthaut translates it as 'sūr' meaning secured or certain.

4r

4r Top

> *You, ashamed for this reason will either perhaps lose your sword or you will lie prostrate on the ground with nothing stopping you.*

The crowned master is depicted as a student in the other treatises. Having deflected an attack from the Long Tail guard, the master hooks his hilt over his opponent's wrist so as to disarm him. The Paris is likely in error in two ways. First, in depicting the victor as a master rather than a scholar, and second, in not showing the hilt over the opponent's wrist.

4r Bottom

> *It is expedient that you hit the ground while your chest has been trampled, and then I will be able to attack you however I want.*[11]

Once more a crowned master is shown, but he is likely a student. The master has deflected his opponent's attack to the side from the Long Tail guard. From here he has wrapped his arm around the opponent's neck. By riding forward, the master will throw his opponent to the ground.

From the Getty MS Ludwig XV 13.

The master in the Long Tail guard.

---

[11] This translation is not completely literal but it's the best way to convey the sense of things.

¶ You, ashamed for this reason will either perhaps lose your sword or you will lie prostrate on the ground with nothing stopping you.

¶ It is expedient that you hit the ground while your chest has been trampled, and then I will be able to attack you however I want.

¶ I protect myself now from a cut and a strong point and I strike the face with my pommel in order that this my sword may not be grabbed, in order that I up till now I may not have been thrown onto the lowest ground.

¶ I will throw you while nothing is stopping your horse, on whose raging haunch my chest will sit, I do not abandon the resonating groans of your horse until you touch the muddy ground headlong with the top of your head, indeed, this best trick is good against an armored man when he is not afraid of anyone striking him in his armor.

4v Top

> *I protect myself now from a cut and a strong point and I strike the face with my pommel in order that this my sword may not be grabbed, in order that I up till now I may not have been thrown onto the lowest ground.*

The crowned master is actually a counter-master defeating the prior plays. The opponent in the Long Tail guard has beat aside the master's sword. In response, the master has brought his pommel around to strike the opponent in the face. While riding past, he can use the false edge of his sword to strike his opponent in the back of the head. This is likely a flick of the sword over the shoulder. While not very powerful, to the back of an unarmored head it is enough. The Paris shows an unusual grip of the sword not like the other treatises and is likely an artistic error.

From the Getty MS Ludwig XV 13.

4v Bottom

> *I will throw you while nothing is stopping your horse,[12] on whose raging[13] haunch my chest will sit, I do not abandon the resonating groans of your horse[14] until you touch the muddy ground headlong with the top of your head, indeed, this best trick[15] is good against an armored man when he is not afraid of anyone striking him in his armor.[16]*

The crowned master has ridden his horse into the flanks of his opponent's. He has reached over the horse's neck and grasped the bridle. By spurring his horse into the opponent's horse, and jerking his arm upwards, he can throw the horse, and rider, to the ground.

12　Illegible annotation above caballuz (horse)
13　Fremitando: from fremitare: to roar, to rage
14　Quadrupedis: literally 'four-footed one'
15　Captio, onis (f.): trick, deception, seizing, apprehension
16　Literally: when he is not afraid that anyone can strike him in his armor.

5r Top

I hold you when you who turn your back have been grabbed by the helmet, I then will send you to the ground from your rushing[17] chest.

The crowned master has ridden up behind his opponent. He has reached out to grab his opponent's helmet, but could have grabbed his shoulder or hair. From here he can throw the opponent. The Getty shows the master as a student and a different grip over the opponent's right shoulder.

From the Getty MS Ludwig XV 13

5r Bottom

There is a way to make sure you strike the ground while your body has been trampled, opposite movements cause this, you nevertheless desired to make this same attempt on me myself.

The crowned master is a counter-master defeating the prior play. The opponent tried to grab the master from behind. In response, the master released the reins of his horse with his left hand and wrapped his arm over the opponent's extended arm, trapping him. The counter-master's right hand meanwhile takes up the reins.

---

17 Currendo: future passive participle/gerundive which seems to be used like a present active participle (currente)

❡ I hold you when you who turn your back have been grabbed by the helmet, I then will send you to the ground from your rushing chest.

❡ There is a way to make sure you strike the ground while your body has been trampled, opposite movements cause this, you nevertheless desired to make this same attempt on me myself.

¶ By raising you from your stable leg this powerful right hand of mine will turn you to the ground, and there will be no limb which may soften the blow.

¶ Look at how I hold your neck with my strong arm; you who were attempting in vain if you were attempting to carry me to the ground while I am unarmed, yet the opposite things defeat you.

5v

5v Top

By raising you from your stable leg[18] this powerful right hand of mine will turn you to the ground, and there will be no limb which may soften the blow.

The crowned master is depicted as a student in the Getty and Morgan, but a master in the Pisani-Dossi. The master has reached down and grabbed his opponent's stirrup. By lifting up, the opponent will fall from the saddle. If the opponent is without stirrups, the play is even easier and can be done by grasping the ankle.

5v Bottom

Look at how I hold your neck with my strong arm; you who were attempting in vain if you were attempting to carry me to the ground while I am unarmed, yet the opposite things defeat you.

The crowned master is a counter-master defeating the prior play. As the opponent dips his waist so as to reach for the counter-master's stirrup, he has wrapped his arm around his neck. The opponent will not be able to reach the stirrup he is after and he in turn will be thrown from his horse as the two steeds ride past.

From the Getty MS Ludwig XV 13

---

18   An alternative translation of this passage is 'from your leg stably' ('stabile' could be an adjective or adverb)

6r Top

If Rolandus, Pulicanus,[19] and harsh Fraxinea[20] should attack me while I am on foot I would delay them by aiming with my spear and let him even hold a javelin in his wild right hand like a club and I would strike more wildly[21] when the spears have been deflected, I will first draw back the high[22] heads of the attackers as soon as possible with this action.

The crowned master of the (heavy spear/ghiavarina) waits in the guard of Boar's Tooth. Three riders are his opponent but he is not fighting them all at once. He will use the same technique for three different attacks. The rider farthest from the foreground has his spear low for an underhanded attack, the other has his held in the middle, while the rider nearest the foreground will throw his spear.

6r Bottom

Now this lance cuts your head when it has been injured by an ample wound and the caution of the proud master influences me.

The crowned master defeats each of the riders, one by one, the same way. His right foot advances a little, he then passes at an angle with the left foot while using his heavy spear to deflect the incoming attacks to his right. The spear's head is brought to the head of the opponent to either thrust or cut. In the Getty version, Fiore notes that this technique could also be used with a staff or sword.

---

19 Above each of these names is written 'nomen proprium' (his own name)
20 There is something illegible written above this name.
21 The word 'furibundior' could have multiple translations: more wildly, more ragingly, more madly
22 Berthaut translates alta as 'fieres' (proud) rather than the literal high.

If Rolandus, Pulicanus, and harsh Fraxinea should attack me while I am on foot I would delay them by aiming with my spear and let him even hold a javelin in his wild right hand like a club and I would strike more wildly when the spears have been deflected, I will first draw back the high heads of the attackers as soon as possible with this action.

Now this lance cuts your head when it has been injured by an ample wound and the caution of the proud master influences me.

¶ Here I cleverly have struck the lips with a hard blow because I expect to procure a wound with the heavy point.

¶ Although I am accustomed to change and to bring back on the opposite side with an outstretched point, I do not delay all things with a short spear.

6v Top

Here I cleverly have struck the lips with a hard blow because I expect to procure a wound with the heavy point.

The garter wearing student has had their spear pushed to the rider's left side. Quickly, the student passes to their left, bringing the butt of their spear around so as to strike the rider in the face. The art depicts the butt of the spear on the left side of the rider, but this is an error and it should be on the right as seen in the Getty version of the Flower of Battle.

From the Getty MS Ludwig XV 13.

6v Bottom

Although I am accustomed to change and to bring back on the opposite side with an outstretched point, I do not delay all things with a short spear.

The crowned master of the spear is in the guard Wide Iron Gate and awaits his opponent. In the Getty version of the Flower of Battle, all the masters of the spear and their opponents are wearing armor, and the target is the face. In the Paris version, the opponents are not wearing armor. The opponents are twisted, so that their heels are facing the master. The Getty is not quite as dramatic, with the heels facing the reader. In either case, the opponent's intent is to unwind their body and drive the spear toward the master.

From the Getty MS Ludwig XV 13.

7r

7r Top

Although my spear can be shorter [23] you nevertheless will leave when you have been pierced and you may throw first if it pleases you in some way, don't flee from there, grievous prizes await you when you have been pierced.

The crowned master of the spear is in the guard Middle Iron Gate and awaits his opponent. From here, the incoming strike will be deflected to the left as the master passes, delivering a thrust. In the Getty, Fiore notes that in any guard with the point offline, when using the short spear or sword, it is possible to deflect and pass with a thrust.

7r Bottom

My spear will now repel your spear[24] by penetrating and I will thrust into your chest with a large wound.

The crowned master of the spear is in Right Window and awaits his opponent. The Getty version has the spear in front of the master's face, which is correct. In the Paris version, the face remains exposed and the spear rests in something more akin to the Woman's Guard. However, it is difficult to perform the play which follows, indicating that this is an error of the artist.

From the Getty MS Ludwig XV 13.

---

23   A more literal translation of 'sit brevior licet hasta michi' would be 'it is permitted for my spear to be shorter'

24   'hasta mea' (my spear) 'tuum telum' (your spear). Both 'hasta' and 'telum' mean spear. The author seems to have used both words in order to fit the meter since both spears appear identical.

¶ Although my spear can be shorter   you nevertheless will leave when you have been pierced and you may throw first if it pleases you in some way, don't flee from there, grievous prizes await you when you have been pierced.

¶ My spear will now repel your spear   by penetrating and I will thrust into your chest with a large wound.

¶ This special thing (MOVEMENT) from the three previous masters fails to strike back, and the motion is to run through the man's chest with a spear or his face and face even quicker with grievous blood.

¶ I mix up counter attacks in order that you may not hurt me more, I compress you by striking your teeth if you are fighting back.

7v Top

> *This special thing (movement) from the three previous masters fails to strike back, and the motion is to run through the man's chest with a spear or his face and face[25] even quicker with grievous blood.*

The crowned remedy master acts from Wide Iron Gate, Middle Iron Gate, or Right Window. When the opponent unwinds his body and thrusts, the master passes forward and to the right, beating aside the opponent's spear, while at the same time delivering their own thrust to the opponent's face. While performing this technique it is possible to slide the spear through the right hand to ensure the point remains on target. At closer ranges this is necessary and is depicted when comparing the previous guard masters and the remedy master.

7v Bottom

> *I mix up counter attacks in order that you may not hurt me more, I compress you by striking your teeth if you are fighting back.[26]*

This is a crowned counter-master who defeats the prior play, but he lacks the garter that is used to indicate counter-masters in the Getty. The counter-master has delivered a thrust, with the right leg leading. Soon as the counter-master's spear is struck off line, he passes and uses the butt of his spear to strike the opponent in the face.

From the Getty MS Ludwig XV 13.

---

25   'faciem' and 'vultus' both mean face. While 'faciem' means 'appearance' more precisely, It is unclear what the distinction between the two is in this context.

26   A more literal translation of this line would be "and I compress you when you are fighting back because your teeth have been struck."

8r Top

In a similar shape I delay you with a dagger and a club,[27] but the club thoroughly blesses[28] me with protection, and this dagger strikes the chest, nevertheless a blade could do everything I do with the club, although we can use better plays than this by moving the easily-moving arms.[29]

In this situation the crowned master is in Wide Iron Gate and has a spear and rondel. The master plants the staff in the ground and tilts it to the right, and adjusts his toes to do the same. When the opponent, armed with a spear, thrusts, the master tilts the spear to the left while turning his feet, also to the left. Once this is done, the opponent's spear will be to the left of the master, who can pass forward and stab the opponent in the chest.

8r Bottom

Here I detain you with two sticks and also a dagger but I will strike first and I will hold this remaining stick[30] covering my limbs with it when we will both come to the close, here I will strike you quickly under your exposed chest with a dagger.

In this situation the crowned master is in an unnamed guard, armed with tree branches, or cudgels. In this clearly self-defense situation, the master hurls the branch in his right hand at the opponent's head as he attacks with the spear. The master then passes, using his left hand, still holding a branch, to cover the spear while he draws a dagger and stabs his opponent in the chest.

---

27   It is unclear why the author uses the word 'clava' (club) when the drawing depicts a spear and a dagger instead of a club and a dagger.
28   The manuscript has not written this word clearly. Berthaut transcribes it as 'perbet' which he translates as 'fournit' (provides). I will take it as 'perbeat' (to thoroughly make happy, to bless) because this word better fits the meter than 'perbet.'
29   Here arms means the body parts, not weapons.
30   In the margins of the text, the two words 'hoc ego' (I, with this) are written in the margin next to the word 'Illo' (with that). Both alternatives fit the meter.

In a similar shape I delay you with a dagger and a club, but the club thoroughly blesses me with protection, and this dagger strikes the chest, nevertheless a blade could do everything I do with the club, although we can use better plays than this by moving the easily-moving arms.

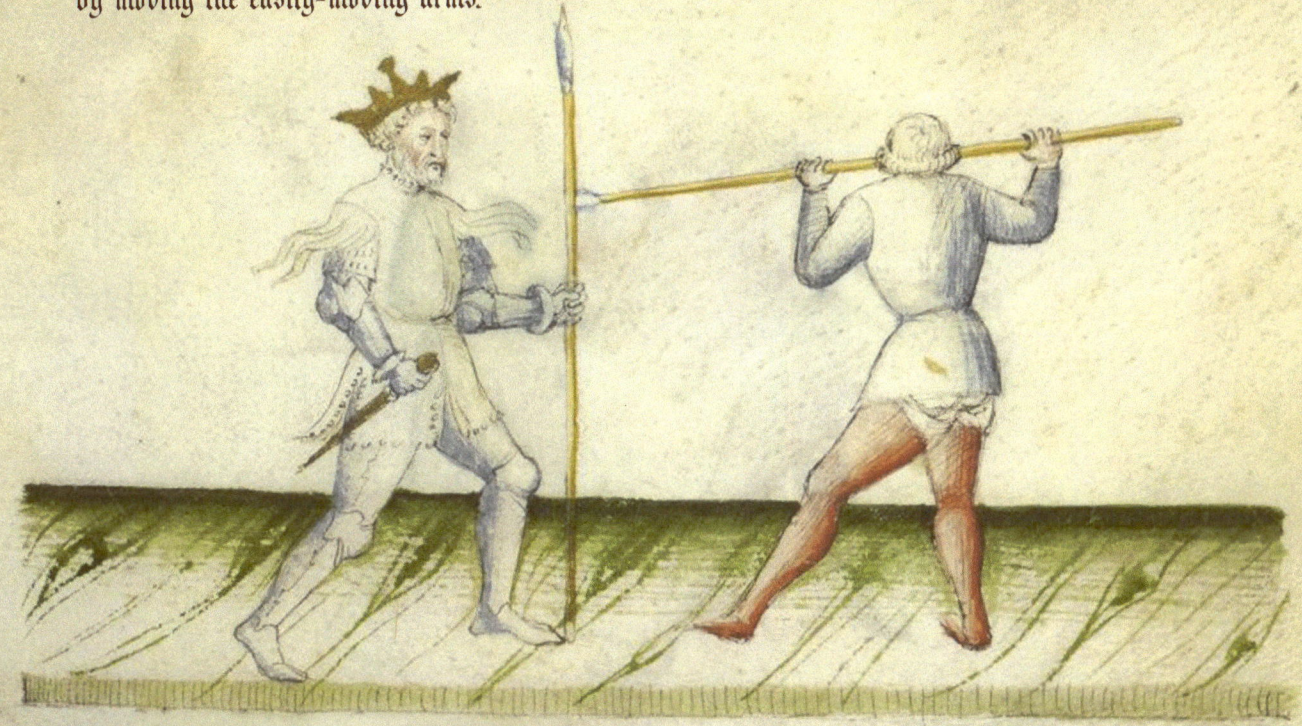

Here I detain you with two sticks and also a dagger but I will strike first and I will hold this remaining stick covering my limbs with it when we will both come to the close, here I will strike you quickly under your exposed chest with a dagger.

¶ I work at this thing in actions which the master now speaks in words, and I fix this dagger under your chest.

¶ Behold, I am called the short position among mortals drawing the spear close in my hands, and if the point should not attempt to deceive me, I would trap you, provided Jupiter is present.

¶ Behold, I am a strong position, and I am called the cross, no strike opposes me, nor yet does any point of the pole-axe oppose me.

8v Top

I work at this thing in actions which the master now speaks in words,[31] *and I fix this dagger under your chest.*

Behold, I am called the short position among mortals drawing the spear close in my hands, and if the point should not attempt to deceive me, I would trap you, provided Jupiter is present.[32]

Here, the student, depicted with a garter, has done as the master had instructed. He has thrown one branch, and passed forward, using his left hand to cover the opponent's spear, while drawing and striking the opponent in the chest. The Getty shows the thrown branch on the ground. The Getty also explains a means to counter the play, in which the spear can be raised, collecting the dagger from below and rotating, presumably to deliver a strike with the butt of the spear.

8v Bottom

Behold, I am a strong position, and I am called the cross, no strike opposes me, nor yet does any point of the pole-axe oppose me.[33]

The crowned master of the axe on the left is in the guard of the Short Serpent. The Getty notes that from this guard, great thrusts can be delivered that can penetrate a breastplate.

The master of the axe on the right is lacking a crown and is in the guard of the True Cross. The Getty indicates that the True Cross of the axe can do the same play as the True Cross from the sword in armor. A cover is made by passing, followed by leveraging the weapon over the opponent's and delivering a thrust.

From the Getty MS Ludwig XV 13.

---

31   Essentially, 'I am putting into practice what the master now describes in words.'

32   The phrase 'Modo Jupiter adsit' ('provided Jupiter is present') essentially means 'if you are lucky.' This is a quotation from Aeneid 3.116. In that line, Aeneas' father Anchises urges the Trojans to sail to Crete and build a settlement there. Anchises and says "placemus ventos et Cnosia regna petamus. Nec longo distant cursu: modo Jupiter adsit," ("Let us please the winds and let us seek the Cretan kingdom. It is not far away provided Jupiter is present.") However, Anchises only wants to sail to Crete because he has misinterpreted Apollo's prophecy at his temple in Delos. By settling in Crete instead of Italy, the Trojans subject themselves to a year-long plague and are forced to leave. It is curious that Fiore would quote Anchises' poor advice when describing the 'breve' (short) position. This may be a commentary on the deceptiveness or riskiness of that position. More likely though, the phrase 'modo Jupiter adsit,' had been divorced from its original Vergilian context by Fiore's time and was simply a common expression for 'if you are lucky.'

33   The Latin term for this weapon is 'tricuspis,' which literally means 'three-points.' The English term for the weapon depicted is a pole-axe.

9r Top

Behold,[34] I am the woman's position, pure of faith, and I create deadly blows by my twin blows.

I am the boar's tooth, strong and terribly bold, not at all do I fear the blows which you make, we confess that it is not possible.

The crowned master of the axe on the left is in Woman's Guard. In the Getty, Fiore says powerful strikes can be delivered by having the left foot move a little off the line. He does not say in which direction, with a wide enough stance, it is possible to move the foot either way and remain stable. To the left opens up his hips, giving more power to the strike, to the right takes you offline from the opponent. After the initial movement of the foot, a pass is taken which powers the strike of the axe toward the head or arms of the opponent. In the Getty, the Woman's Guard is opposed to the Boar's Tooth.

The crowned master of the axe on the right is in Boar's Tooth. The Getty refers to this guard as the Middle Iron Gate, even though the prior play says otherwise. It is also mentioned that the two guards have faced one another many times before. From here, a powerful strike is awaited. The front foot moves off the line, likely to the left, without crossing the feet, while the poleaxe is driven upwards and to the right with a deflection. The opponent's poleaxe will be knocked aside, allowing for a pass and strike to the head. In the Getty, the play is described using a longsword against the poleaxe, in which case, after the deflection, a pass is taken and the sword gripped in the middle of the blade with the left hand, so a thrust can be deliver to the face.

9r Bottom

Your pole-axe[35] has indeed been thrown onto the ground, but mine will strike your face with a heavy wound.

The crowned remedy master has beaten the opponent's axe to the ground while passing forward. The Getty notes that from here several plays are possible. The opponent is shown without armor, but all other version of the Flower of Battle depict all the men using the poleaxe in armor.

---

34 'pro ecce' is written on top of 'en,' which is an exhortation. 'Pro ecce' is another exhortation.
35 See Footnote 33.

❡ Behold, I am the woman's position, pure of faith, and I create deadly blows by my twin blows.

❡ I am the boar's tooth, strong and terribly bold, not at all do I fear the blows which you make, we confess that it is not possible.

❡ Your pole-axe has indeed been thrown onto the ground, but mine will strike your face with a heavy wound.

❡ Now I have burst forth suddenly from the boar's tooth and by my own pole-axe, and I have struck those sinews of the face.

❡ Behold, I press your face with a strong hand, and you feel that, and now this sacred pole-axe of mine draws out your teeth.

9v Top

Now I have burst forth suddenly[36] from the boar's tooth and by my own pole-axe,[37] and I have struck those sinews of the face.

The crowned person is shown as a remedy master, but is shown as a student in the Getty version. The Getty also explains the play as a possible follow up to a previous play that is not shown in the Paris version. The Getty suggests stepping on the opponent's poleaxe once it is brought to the ground, and pulling back so as to stab the opponent in the face, similar to the breaking of the thrust technique shown in the sword in two hands section. The Pisani Dossi and Morgan indicate this a play to be done from Boar's Tooth, and not from a crossing.

From the Getty MS Ludwig XV 13.

9v Bottom

Behold, I press your face with a strong hand, and you feel that, and now this sacred pole-axe of mine[38] draws out your teeth.[39]

The crowned person is also shown as a remedy master, but in other versions is shown as a garter-wearing student. The play is to be done if the opponent's face is not a viable target due to armor. The left foot is advanced and the left hand opens the opponent's visor, while the right hand stabs the poleaxe into the opponent's face. The Paris version shows the opponent out of armor, and so the technique makes little sense, but was likely an artistic choice.

From the Getty MS Ludwig XV 13.

---

36   'Id est subito' (it is sudden) is above 'presto' (Berthaut).
37   See footnote 33.
38   'Vel tibi' (or yours) is written above 'mea' (my/of mine) (Berthaut).
39   See footnote 33.

10r Top

In this disarm I will strongly perform a twist. Here your pole-axe will be lost but my pole-axe[40] will strike you in the front provided that the fates want to assist a powerful man.[41]

The crowned person, like before, is depicted as a remedy master, but in other versions is a student. While the right foot is leading, in the Getty it is the left, but the play works either way. The play is to be done at close range by abandoning the weapon and seeking the opponent's. The opponent's poleaxe is grabbed on either side of his hands. A sharp turn is made clockwise while passing back to wrench the opponent's poleaxe free. In the Getty the follow up is to strike the opponent in the head with his own weapon. The play is similar to a play in the Getty with the longsword.

From the Getty MS Ludwig XV 13.

10r Bottom

Whether the savage sword is thrown or prepares to cleave, another may still desire me alone with the point; This defense teaches so that by not laughing, I may not be afraid.

Here, three opponents face a master in an unnamed guard of the sword in one hand. He is back-weighted drawing in his opponent. This is also the start of the remedy, making this both a guard and remedy master. The opponents are to attack one at a time. One is going to throw his sword, another cut, and another is going to thrust. The play starts off the same no matter what is done. The front foot moves a little forward and to the left or right off the line while the sword is used to deflect, parry or break the attack. A step to the left exposes the outside of the opponent, such as their elbow, while a step to the right exposes their inside, such as their wrist. From there a pass is taken and various plays can be performed.

---

40   See footnote 33.
41   This is a way of saying 'if I am lucky.'

¶ In this disarm I will strongly perform a twist. Here your pole-axe will be lost but my pole-axe will strike you in the front provided that the fates want to assist a powerful man.

¶ Whether the savage sword is thrown or prepares to cleave, another may still desire me alone with the point; This defense teaches so that by not laughing, I may not be afraid.

By making a pass with my raging sword I cover my limbs. From there I will penetrate your chest with that sword.

In order that I may strike you again with the point, my left hand holds this mournful sword with strength.

10v Top

> *B*y making a pass with my raging sword I cover my limbs. From there I will penetrate your chest with that sword.

The student has moved their front foot to the right while beating aside the incoming attack. A pass is taken so they can drive their point into the opponent's chest. The distance is still great enough that the left hand does not have to be involved.

10v Bottom

> *I*n order that I may strike you again with the point, my left hand holds this mournful sword with strength.

The student has moved their front foot to the right while beating aside the attack. The student follows up with a pass and a thrust aimed at the chest, using their left hand on the middle of their own sword. The Getty version suggests this technique be done in armor. As can be seen, the opponent's sword is free and could cause trouble to an unarmored foe.

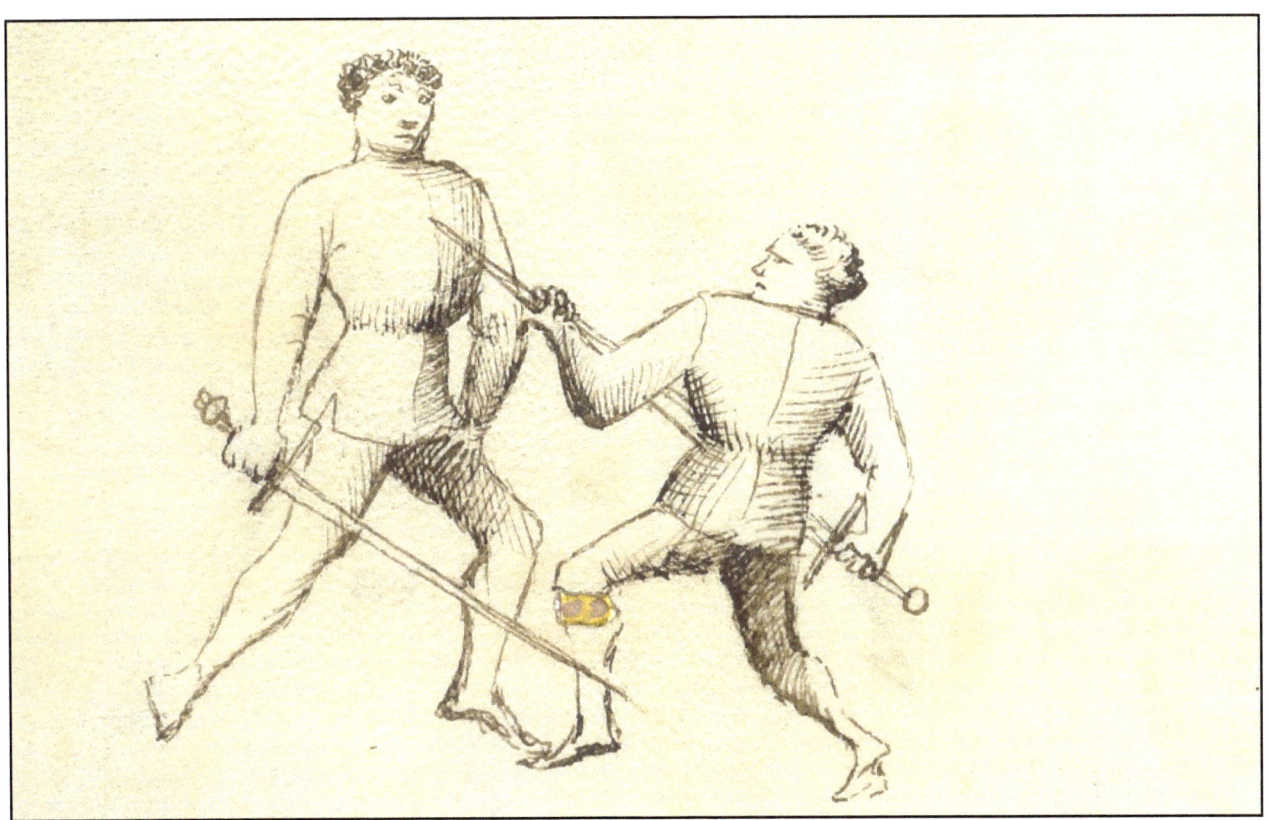

From the Getty MS Ludwig XV 13.

11r Top

*H*ere I have struck your chest with a bloody wound because I have covered myself with a quick defense while giving this.

The student has moved their front foot to the right while covering the attack. A hanging parry can do this. A pass is then taken, and the blade is rotated to strike at the opponent, while on the inside of their sword. The Getty version is different and implies no passing step is needed, but instead a rotation of the body and strike, hitting the opponent before they can act, or deflecting the opponent's attack and then striking. Note in the Getty version the student's sword is on the outside.

From the Getty MS Ludwig XV 13.

11r Bottom

*L*augh at me and call me blind with your voice if this sword of yours which I clearly grab by the hilt does not fall into the ground then remain exposed.

The student has moved his front foot to the right while beating aside the opponent's attack. A pass is then taken and the left hand grabs the opponent's hand and hilt. While in other versions, the hand is thumb down and the grip is to the inside to allow a twist, in this case, the thumb is pointed up and the grip is on the outside indicating a possible artistic error. After the grab is made the student's sword is drawn back for a thrust.

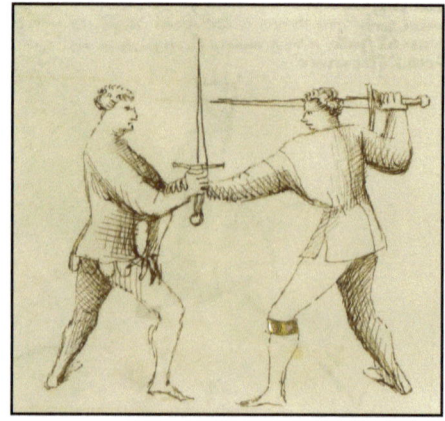

From the Getty MS Ludwig XV 13.

Here I have struck your chest with a bloody wound because I have covered myself with a quick defense while giving this.

Laugh at me and call me blind with your voice if this sword of yours which I clearly grab by the hilt does not fall into the ground then remain exposed.

⁋ I expose you in order that I may strike you with an outstretched point. After this we will perfectly make a defense with an intent to destroy.

⁋ I decide to snatch your sword from your slow hands, this more skillful hand snatched it from you in such a way.

11v:

11v top

> *I expose you in order that I may strike you with an outstretched point. After this we will perfectly[42] make a defense with an intent to destroy.[43]*

A counter-master is depicted with a crown and garter, even though in other versions of the Flower of Battle he is just another student. The front foot has moved to the right and the attack has been beat aside. A pass is taken, and the left hand has reached forward. From there, it is possible to push the opponent's blade to the left, or grip their wrist, while a thrust is delivered toward their face.

From the Getty MS Ludwig XV 13.

11v bottom

> *I decide to snatch your sword from your slow hands, this more skillful hand snatched it from you in such a way.*

The student, wearing a garter, has moved his front foot, likely to the right to gain access to the opponent's outside, all while beating aside an attack. The student has then passed and his left hand has gripped the opponent's hilt of the sword below their hand on the outside. In other versions of the Flower of Battle the grip is to the inside with the thumb down to allow a twisting motion. In the Paris version the grip is to the outside and thumb up. As in previous plays, a thrust is leveled at the opponent's face and is on the inside of their sword.

From the Getty MS Ludwig XV 13.

---

42   This is an idiom which literally means 'to the fingernail/toenail.'
43   This is an idiom which literally means 'with a crushing soul/mind.'

12r Top

Now I think that I have slit the middle of the throat with the blade, because I have turned around this elbow here.

This play is unique to the Paris version of the Flower of Battle in that the opponent is resisting with a rondel. The likely play is that the student's front foot moves far to the right while the opponent's attack is deflected. A pass is then made where his left leg is placed behind the opponent's lead leg and a push is given to their elbow, followed by wrapping the sword around the opponent's neck to cut his throat or throw him to the ground.

There is some similarities to the Getty and Pisani Dossi versions of the Flower of Battle in which the opponent is pushed by the elbow and turned. At this point the student flings his sword around the opponent's neck, and then grabs his own blade.

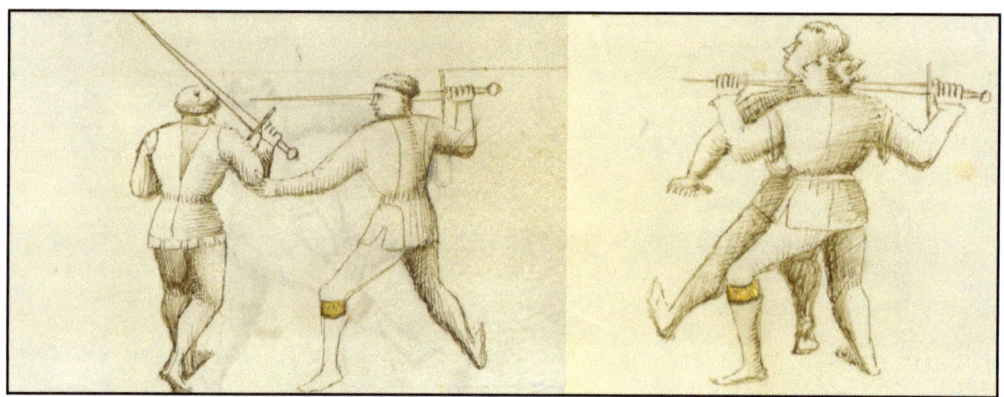

From the Getty MS Ludwig XV 13.

12r Bottom

And when I twist your elbow with my hand I will, while twisting, make you bloody with my blade, I cannot deceive.

The student wearing a garter has moved his front foot to the left while covering with his sword, this has exposed the opponent's elbow. A pass is taken and the student pushes with his left hand to turn the opponent, while drawing back his sword for a thrust. In the Paris version, the sword remains on the inside of the opponent's, but in the Getty the sword has been drawn far enough back to be free of the turning opponent.

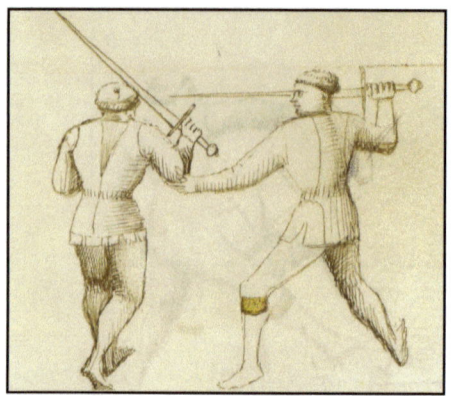

From the Getty MS Ludwig XV 13.

❡ Now I think that I have slit the middle of the throat with the blade, because I have turned around this elbow here.

❡ And when I twist your elbow with my hand I will, while twisting, make you bloody with my blade, I cannot deceive.

¶ Each position and guard calls deceptively by its name. One is similar and yet contrary to the other, thus even here we seize similar actions by their position.

¶ I, who always on every side recover equally from cuts and thrusts, am called the earthly iron door.

¶ I am the daring high woman's position, and I defend only the high limbs of a raging man to whatever place.

¶ I am indeed the regal position of the true window and I confess that I am always quick in the famous art.

¶ I am called the strong middle iron door, and I give heavy blows, and I seek death with the point.

12v

12v Top

Each position and guard calls[44] deceptively by its name. One is similar and yet contrary to the other, thus even here we seize similar actions by their position.

I, who always on every side recover equally from cuts and thrusts,[45] am called the earthly iron door.

I am the daring high woman's position, and I defend only[46] the high limbs of a raging man to whatever place.

The crowned master of the sword in two hands on the left is in the guard of Iron Gate. The stance is very broad, allowing for numerous techniques. The Getty says from this guard it is possible to cover and pass into the narrow plays, or exchange thrusts.

The crowned master of the sword in two hands on the right is in the Woman's Guard. The stance is back-weighted and held very high and is one of many variations of the Woman's Guard to be found in Fiore's works. From here thrusts can be broken and powerful attacks can be launched.

12v bottom

I am indeed the regal position of the true window and I confess that I am always quick in the famous art.

I am called the strong middle iron door, and I give heavy blows, and I seek death with the point.

The crowned master of the sword in two hands on the left is in the Window on the Right guard. In the Paris version the guard is drawn incorrectly with the sword behind the head so as to not obscure the face. This is the same artistic choice, or error, made in the depiction of the Window on the Right with the spear.

The crowned master of the sword in two hands on the right is in the Middle Iron Gate guard. The Getty describes how it is possible to deflect incoming attacks upward and return with powerful cuts. The guard is also good at delivering strong thrusts.

---

44   'Scilicet nobis' (it is clear to us) is written above 'vocat' (calls)
45   A more literal translation would be 'from blows of a cut and of the point.'
46   Modo: can be translated multiple ways but 'only' is the most likely one.

13r:

13r Top

I remain with a short sword, but nevertheless here I am named long, most often suited to cutting the throat.[47]

I myself am called the useful frontal crown position, I do not spare anything when I break with a cut or with the point.

The crowned master of the sword in two hands on the left is in the Long guard. The Getty describes the Long guard as deceptive, able to deliver thrusts, avoid blows and respond with its own.

The crowned master of the sword in two hands on the right is in the Front guard. The Getty describes this guard extensively. It is able to cross with attacks, including exchanging the point from high thrusts, or breaking the thrust against low thrusts. Another technique is to pass backwards from a low thrust and deliver a cut toward the opponent's head or arms, transitioning to Boar's Tooth and then advancing with thrusts.

13r Bottom

I am the woman's position opposed to the boar's tooth bearing obstacles in many ways from the skilled chest.[48]

I am the boar's position, daring and huge in my strength, experienced at revealing strength to all defenses.

The crowned master of the sword in two hands on the left is in another variation of the Woman's Guard. From here it is possible to deliver powerful cuts, but also to raise the arms and deliver a cunning thrust.

The crowned master of the sword in two hands on the right is in the guard of Boar's Tooth. In the Getty version Fiore spends more time on this guard than any other. To begin with, the guard can remain stationary and deliver powerful thrusts toward an opponent's face. The guard can advance the front foot, deliver a thrust, and then return the foot. The guard is also able to thwart opponents seeking narrow plays.

---

47   I took some liberties in translating this phrase. A more literal translation would be 'most often cutting the throat with my nature.'

48   Berthaut claims that due to a scribal error, the phrase could either be 'impedimenta ferens versuto pectore multis' (bearing obstacles in many ways from the skilled chest) or 'impedimenta ferens versuto pectore multa' (bearing many obstacles from the skilled chest); 'scilicet' (clearly) has been written illegibly above 'versuto' (skilled).

¶ I remain with a short sword, but nevertheless here I am named long, most often suited to cutting the throat.

¶ I myself am called the useful frontal crown position, I do not spare anything when I break with a cut or with the point.

¶ I am the woman's position opposed to the boar's tooth bearing obstacles in many ways from the skilled chest.

¶ I am the boar's position, daring and huge in my strength, experienced at revealing strength to all defenses.

¶ Here I am the shorter position, and I repel the long sword. I often threaten with the point, nevertheless, I return to there from there.

¶ I myself am called the raised position of the true window, thus I am quick on this right and certainly on the left.

¶ Behold, I am the tailed position dragged forth/ brought forth onto the ground. And I very often lead blows before and after blows that have been thrown across.

¶ I certainly am named the two-horned position by everyone, don't ask how deceptive nor how clever I am against you.

13v:

13v Top

Here I am the shorter position, and I repel the long sword. I often threaten with the point, nevertheless, I return to there from there.[49]

I myself[50] *am called the raised position of the true window, thus I am quick on this right and certainly on the left.*

The crowned master of the sword in two hands on the left is in the Short guard. In the Getty, Fiore notes that the Short guard has to stay moving, can perform great thrusts, and is better used while in armor. This is because the guard offers little else. While it can exchange a thrust or deliver one, it cannot easily cut, and while the Long guard can retract to avoid a blow, the Short guard has nowhere to retract to.

The crowned master of the sword in two hands on the right is in the Woman's Guard on the left although it is misnamed the raised position of the Window in the Paris. This guard, like the other variations of the Woman's Guard can perform powerful strikes. In the Getty, Fiore notes that this guard can also be used to get to the narrow plays.

13v Bottom

Behold, I am the tailed position dragged forth/brought forth onto the ground. And I very often lead blows before and after blows that have been thrown across.

I certainly am named the two-horned position by everyone, don't ask how deceptive nor how clever I am against you.

The crowned master of the sword in two hands on the left is in the Long Tail guard. The Getty notes that this guard is good for waiting in, can deliver thrust, covers and strikes and also can transition to other guards easily. Additionally, when passing and cutting, the guard can be used to get to the narrow plays.

The crowned master of the sword in two hands on the right is in the Two-Horned guard. This is an unusual guard in that it is depicted very differently in the various versions of the Flower of Battle. The Paris has one of the clearest illustrations. The guard is very strong in the center, and so long as the point is directed at the opponent's face, is very difficult to push aside. It can deliver strong thrusts and according to Fiore can also do what the Long guard can do.

---

49   Berthaut adds some interpretation so his translation reads "là (court) je retourne cependant de là (long, pointe)" (from there (the short position) I nevertheless return to there (long point).

50   This is the first occurrence in the text of the intensive pronoun/adjective ipse, ipsa, ipsum. As an adjective, it intensifies the noun it modifies but as a pronoun it can mean 'I myself,' 'you yourself,' 'he himself,' 'she herself,' 'it itself.' This word appears a total of twenty times in this text. Berthaut shows us that on pages 13V, 22R, 30R, 33R, 38V, 40V, 41V, and 42R, the text owner annotated the text with either 'scilicet ego' ('clearly, I') (13V, 22R, 33R, 40V, 41V), 'ego' ('I') (30R), 'scilicet tu' (clearly, you) (40V), and 'tu scilicet' (you clearly) (42R). These are probably the text owner's annotations to remind him of the context-specific translation of ipse, ipsa, ipsum. See footnote 51 for more on the use of the word 'scilicet' in annotations.

14r Top

I hold a compressed space in the bind with my point, but from the other side I weigh down your chest with a heavy point.

The crowned masters are forming a crossing and are in a bind. The Paris is different than other versions of the Flower of Battle which depict three crossings, one at the tip, one at the middle, and one near the guard. In the Getty, for example, the crossing of the tips and middle of the swords are shown at the start of the wide plays. Furthermore, the left foot is leading and only one of the people are shown as a crowned remedy master. The Paris shows what is a crossing near the middle of the blade, but they are far apart and with the right leg leading. Both men depicted are wearing crowns which indicates either can perform the follow up plays.

From the Getty MS Ludwig XV 13. Crossing of the tips and crossing of the middle.

14r Bottom

When the speech of my previous master has been heard, the wild point of the blade approaches the soft throat.

The garter wearing student has performed a play in which, at the crossing of the tips of the sword, finding the opponent weak in the bind, a thrust to the face is performed. In the Getty, this is a play to be done from the crossing of the tips, but in the Paris, a more generalized crossing is depicted for wide plays. An alternative to this play is if the opponent is strong in the bind, to cut them on the other side of the crossing by drawing the sword back. The opponent's blade, having nothing to push against, goes sideways.

I hold a compressed space in the bind with my point, but from the other side I weigh down your chest with a heavy point.

When the speech of my previous master has been heard, the wild point of the blade approaches the soft throat.

¶ I, cleverly holding the sword now in the middle of the sword, will certainly strike your right arm as in the bind, although this time might be much too short for showing these things as much as you wish.

¶ I strike you just as that previous master said before, who holds back the blade in the bind by means of which he may be able to deceive.

14v:

14v Top

I, cleverly holding the sword now in the middle of the sword, will certainly strike your right arm as in the bind, although this time might be much too short for showing these things as much as you wish.

The crowned remedy masters are at a crossing that could be seen as the start of a wide play, or narrow. The master on the left has his left leg leading, which makes sense for wide plays. The master on the right has his right leg leading, which makes sense for narrow plays. The follow up plays are a mix of both wide and narrow. The order is likely mixed up, with this crossing belonging where 14r top is and that one being placed here.

From the Getty MS Ludwig XV 13. Crossing near the guard.

14v Bottom

I strike you just as that previous master said before, who holds back the blade in the bind by means of which he may be able to deceive. [51]

The student on the left has found himself at a crossing with his left leg leading. The bind was strong and so the student has passed, running his sword down the opponent's arm and hands and delivering a thrust to the body. The Paris depicts much more perspective in this play compared to the Getty where it appears the student has passed directly forward and not around the opponent.

From the Getty MS Ludwig XV 13.

---

51   'Scilicet dixit' ('clearly, he said') is written on top of 'tulit' (said). The manuscript owner often (12V, 13R, 13V, 14V, 17V, 22R, 23R, 32R, 33R, 38V, 40V, 41V) writes 'scilicet X' (clearly, X) on top of words in the manuscript where X is a more recognizable synonym for the word that it is written in the manuscript. Since the manuscript's 'tulit' can mean many things besides 'said,' the annotation 'scilicet dixit' reminds us to translate 'tulit' as 'said' since 'dixit' is a more common Latin word for 'said.'

15r[52]

15r Top

If suddenly I[53] turn my sword during a play, I am able to hurt your head in the same way as your hands during the play.

The garter wearing student on the left has exchanged the point of a thrust and delivered his own to the opponent's face. To do this, he awaited with the left leg leading. As the opponent thrust, the student's left foot moved to the right, without crossing his legs, while his sword moved to the left, hands low and tip high. This takes the student off the line, while directing the opponent's thrust away. A pass is then taken so that the student's thrust is driven into the face of his opponent as shown. The Getty is more clear in showing the crossguard protecting the hand than the Paris in which it appears the crossguard is not used at all.

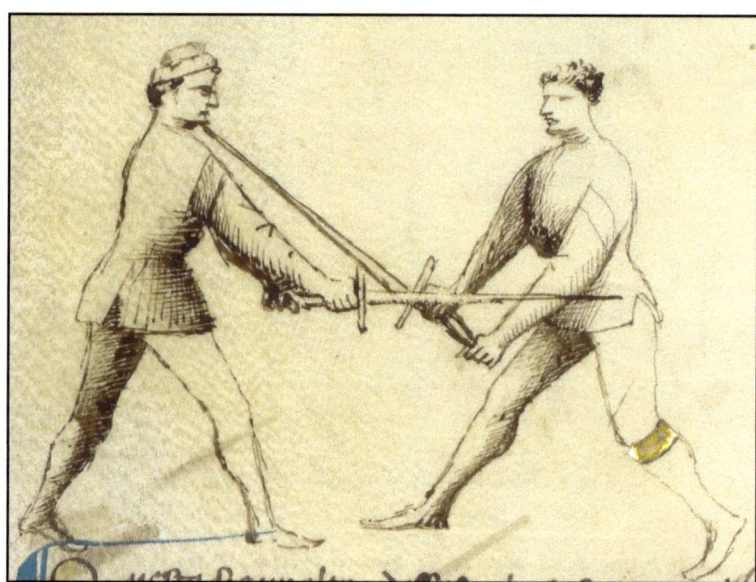

From the Getty MS Ludwig XV 13.

15r Bottom

If you should hold me however you like with your hands, which has come before,[54] I would strike you with this point while cutting your bleeding face.

The garter wearing student exchanged the point of a thrust too far to his left. Unable to pass forward and drive the point of his sword into his opponent's face, he instead has reached over his own sword and grasped the opponent's hilt. Now, with his sword free, the student can draw his arm back and thrust the opponent. If the opponent tries to yank their sword free, this only helps the student with their action.

---

52   The word 'punta' is used to mean thrust on 15V instead of the previous 'ictus cuspidis' used on 12V.
53   Here the author uses the first person plural (we turn) to mean the first person singular (I turn). This was not uncommon in Latin verse.
54   The author appears to have used the interrogative 'quid' (what?) instead of the relative 'quod' (which) by mistake. This phrase 'quod proderitur' (which has come before) refers to the previous drawing.

If suddenly I turn my sword during a play, I am able to hurt your head in the same way as your hands during the play.

If you should hold me however you like with your hands, which has come before, I would strike you with this point while cutting your bleeding face.

Here we now remain in the shape of a cross while fighting. The one who knows more things will always have victorious plays.

Now let your faithless hand suddenly bring forth a thrust through the ground. Here I will strike you straight away with a high wound.

15v Top

> *Here we now remain in the shape of a cross while fighting. The one who knows more things will always have victorious plays.*

The garter wearing student has broken the thrust of an opponent. An exchange works best against a low thrust, while a break against a high. The student waited for the thrust while in a high guard, such as Woman's guard with their left leg leading. As the opponent thrust, the student moved his lead left leg to the right, without crossing his feet. At the same time, the student used the strong of his blade to push the incoming thrust to his left. From here he passed and struck hard and down toward the middle of the opponent's blade. Contact with the blade is not broken, and the cut must be directed at the middle of the opponent's sword so as to drive it to the ground. All together, two actions are taken, though quite a bit goes on during it.

15v Bottom

> *Now let your faithless hand suddenly bring forth a thrust through the ground. Here I will strike you straight away with a high wound.*

The garter wearing student has already broken the thrust of an opponent by striking the middle of their sword. He has then extended his right foot to step on the opponent's blade. From here, a false edge cut can be safely delivered to the neck of the opponent without fear of reprisal.

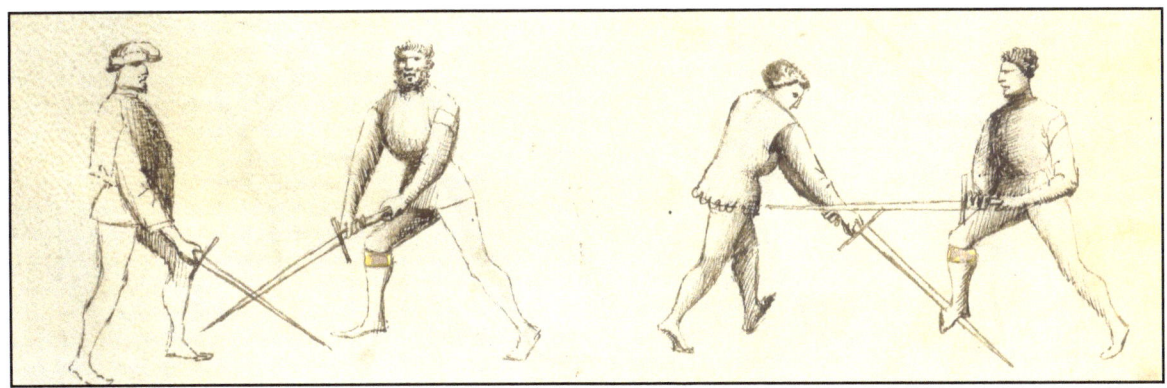

From the Getty MS Ludwig XV 13.

16r Top

I hold my blade above your neck, and you feel this, now you will suffer the work of death, the fates will not deny.

This play derives from armored combat, as shown in the other treatises even though in the Paris version neither opponent is wearing armor. The opponent was too close and so the student has passed, placing his left foot behind their opponent's, while wrapping his sword around the opponent's neck and holding onto it. The student will pass again, so that the right leg is leading, and use his sword and the movement of the pass to throw the opponent to the ground.

From the Getty MS Ludwig XV 13.

16r bottom

From the further right part your sword will fall to the left if I roll myself quickly but when the limbs have previously been pressed together.

This play derives from armored combat as well, despite neither wearing any. The student with the garter is again too close and so seeks a grapple. The sword is taken at the half sword and the point placed under the opponent's right arm. This can be done with a pass or not, so long as the left leg is leading. From here, the student presses close and slips his left hand under the opponent's right arm and seeks a lower lock or throw, seeking out the opponent's triceps.

The lower lock.

I hold my blade above your neck, and you feel this, now you will suffer the work of death, the fates will not deny.

From the further right part your sword will fall to the left if I roll myself quickly but when the limbs have previously been pressed together.

¶ You can feel how great the wound that I shall have crushed your hand with is, and I might be able to strike you with the pommel at the same time.

¶ Here I certainly strike you on the hand so that a bind may occur for me, who looks down on esoteric arms.

16v Top

You can feel how great the wound that I shall have crushed your hand[55] with is, and I might be able to strike you with the pommel at the same time.

This play is from armored combat and is performed from the guard of the Leopard or the True Cross shown later in the manuscript. The student with the garter has passed forward and from the half sword and has pushed aside the opponent's thrust. He is using his blade to press into the opponent's lead hand. From here, the student could drive his pommel into the opponent's face. The Getty depicts this play but reversed, with the other man winning by delivering a thrust to the face. The Morgan shows this play, but it looks like the Paris.

The Leopard guard and the Getty version of the play, in which the other man wins the exchange with a thrust.

16v Bottom

Here I certainly strike you on the hand[56] so that a bind may occur for me, who looks down on esoteric[57] arms.

The garter wearing student is continuing with the play from before. Instead of destroying the opponent's hand, he has pushed hard and is preparing to strike his opponent in the face with the pommel of his sword. The Getty shows a slightly different variation, with the cross-guard being used against the opponent's head.

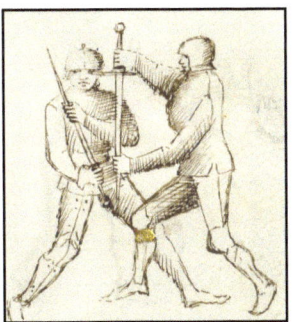

From the Getty MS Ludwig XV 13.

---

55   'id est manum' (that is the hand) is written on top of 'palmaz' (hand). Although they are synonyms, 'manum' is a more common word than 'palmam' so the text's owner must have annotated 'manum' to remind himself what 'palmam' means.
56   'in' (on) is written on top of 'manu' (hand), which completes the meaning 'in manu' (on the hand).
57   'esoteric' is my translation of the Latin word 'grandia.' This word can mean anything from 'large' or 'high' to 'sublime.' I took the word to mean arrogant or obscure so I thought 'esoteric' was a good translation.

17r Top

> Because I am learned in my art I will twist you onto the ground from your backwards-bent chest, from there I will pierce you with the point when you have been cut down.

This play is a continuation of the prior one from 16v. The student has struck the opponent in the face and is preparing to throw him. Note that the student's sword is on the outside of his opponent's.

17r Bottom

> Whether you will leave your own sword from the left part, or whether you would go onto the ground when you have been cut down, you will not deny that it is possible.

This play is an alternative following 16v. The student has struck the opponent in the face and is now preparing to throw him. The pommel is hooked to the opponent's arm. The student can rotate hard and to the right to throw his opponent to the ground. Note that the student's sword is on the inside of his opponent's.

The play of 16v.

Because I am learned in my art I will twist you onto the ground from your backwards-bent chest, from there I will pierce you with the point when you have been cut down.

Whether you will leave your own sword from the left part, or whether you would go onto the ground when you have been cut down, you will not deny that it is possible.

¶This capture certainly makes me safe from your sword. Indeed my sword is free but your sword stays immobilized, and the sword performs the play which is considered the fourth, just as everyone will see easily from the art of bearing the two-edged ax.

¶You will indeed go away because you have been laid low by a lower bind, and I will strike your chest with a lethal wound.

17v Top

This capture certainly makes me safe[58] from your sword. Indeed my[59] sword is free but your sword stays immobilized,[60] and the sword performs the play which is considered the fourth, just as everyone will see easily from the art of bearing the two-edged ax.

The garter wearing student is in fact a counter-master when looking at the instructions of the other versions of the Flower of Battle. The Morgan in particular calls this play out as a counter to the prior ones. If the opponent comes to the close with a cover from the Leopard guard or True Cross, then the response is for the counter-master to use his left hand to grasp and push the right forearm of his opponent. The opponent is thus immobilized allowing the counter-master to draw his sword back and deliver a thrust to the face. He could also give a hard push with his left arm to turn the opponent and possibly throw him.

17v Bottom

You will indeed go away because you have been laid low by a lower bind, and I will strike your chest with a lethal wound.

The garter wearing student has entered the lower lock. His left arm has entered under the opponent's right arm. The student has passed behind his opponent. Here, the left hand should try and grip the triceps and draw inwards toward the chest. At the same time, the right hand of the student goes low so his blade's point can be directed at the opponent. The play is also used as a defense against the dagger, in armored combat, and can be applied anytime the opponent's arms are bent in such a way the left hand can go under the right arm at the joint.

The lower lock against the dagger.

---

58 'Scilicet me' (certainly me) is above tutum (Berthaut). This completes the meaning of 'ense tuo tutum facit hec captura' (this capture *certainly* makes *me* safe from your sword). The word 'me' can be implied but the text's owner included this annotation to facilitate his reading.

59 'scilicet ensis' (certainly sword) is above 'meus' (Berthaut). This completes the meaning of 'nempe meus liber' (indeed *certainly* my *sword* is free). Once again, the text's owner annotated the text to facilitate reading.

60 The literal translation for the word 'carcere' would be 'under imprisonment.'

18r Top

I am called the high serpent, and with my high point I place my limbs under the lowest plane.

*And in the position of the leopard indeed I observe you closely when you are calm, always sending back cuts and the **deepest**[61] blows of the point.[62]*

The crowned master on the left is in the guard of the Raised Serpent. He is holding the sword in the half sword position. From here, the master can pass and with a swinging motion, bring his sword in for a powerful thrust, as if he were using a battering ram. The guard can also be used to push aside thrusts and cuts. In the other versions of the Flower of Battle this is a guard to be used in armor, while in the Paris manuscript the master is shown only partially armored and his counterpart wears none at all.

The crowned master on the right is in the guard of Leopard. The other manuscripts refer to this guard as that of the True Cross. This guard was also intended to be used while wearing armor.

18r Bottom

Now you would think to repel anyone with this guard when, for instance, you will see the students play.

The crowned master has moved from the guard of the Leopard with an angled pass to intercept the opponent's blade. From this position, various follow up plays derive. As before, the guard is for one in armor.

---

61   The author wrote 'ima' (deepest) when he should have written 'imas' (deepest).
62   Here the writer uses 'ictus cuspidis,' (blow of the point) like on 12V, instead of 'punta' (thrust) as written in 15V.

❡ I am called the high serpent, and with my high point I place my limbs under the lowest plane.

❡ And in the position of the leopard indeed I observe you closely when you are calm, always sending back cuts and the deepest blows of the point.

❡ Now you would think to repel anyone with this guard when, for instance, you will see the students play.

❡ From the guard this deepest point of the master leaves and I will make other plays if indeed it is pleasing.

❡ Having been laid low on the ground by the point of the blade you will go away and I will do worse things to you if I feel like it.

18v Top

From the guard this deepest point of the master leaves and I will make other plays if indeed it is pleasing.

The garter wearing student has moved from the guard of the Leopard with a pass, pushing aside the opponent's thrust and delivering one of his own to the opponent's throat. The technique can also be performed from the Bastard Cross.

The Bastard Cross guard.

18v Bottom

Having been laid low on the ground by the point of the blade you will go away and I will do worse things to you if I feel like it.[63]

The garter wearing student is continuing from the prior play. The thrust has been prevented, and so the student places his left foot behind his opponent's. With a hard rotation to the left, the student can use his sword as a lever to throw the opponent over his left leg.

---

63 A more literal translation of this phrase would be "if it will sit in my mind."

19r:

This page is blank.

19r

In the Paris version of the Flower of battle, page 19r was left blank. In its stead I have provided a close up view of different images of the longsword with attention to the way the hands hold the sword. Rather than one particular way, it appears that there was a choice of how exactly to grip a sword based on the user's preference and the guard in question.

¶ We are six very skillful actions in the actions of armor, which any master will perform in armor, from which he will overcome a sword or a dagger and a double-edged ax.

¶ I myself am the short position, and I am called serpentine under the correct name, learned moreover in piercing with the point.

¶ I am a position and I am correctly called the cross by many masters, the point does not hurt me nor will the cut itself hurt.

¶ Here the blade will change into a position that is wicked in its piercing, for I hold my limbs raised in strong armor.

¶ I indeed have been established as the standing middle iron door. I do not hurt with the point too much, but I am always useless.

19v:

19v Top

We are six very skillful actions in the actions of armor, which any master will perform in armor, from which he will overcome a sword or a dagger and a double-edged ax.

I myself am the short position, and I am called serpentine under the correct name, learned moreover in piercing with the point.

I am a position and I am correctly called the cross by many masters, the point does not hurt me nor will the cut itself hurt.

The crowned master on the left is in the guard of the Short Serpent. From here he can deliver thrusts. The guard is for armored combat.

The crowned master on the right is in the guard of the Bastard Cross. The Getty indicates the Bastard Cross can do all the same things as the True (Called Leopard in the Paris), including cover, cut, thrust and avoid strikes by stepping offline. The guard was to be used while wearing armor.

19v Bottom

Here the blade will change into a position that is wicked in its piercing, for I hold my limbs raised in[64] strong armor.[65]

I indeed have been established as the standing middle iron door.[66] I do not hurt with the point too much, but I am always useless.

The crowned master on the left is in the guard of the Archer. From here great thrusts can be delivered as well as covers against incoming attacks. This is also a guard intended to be used while wearing armor. They Getty depicts the guard differently, holding, rather than cradling the blade.

The crowned master on the right is in the guard of Middle Iron Gate. This is the same guard seen in 12v. As with many armored guards, this one can deliver powerful thrusts and can also deflect attacks upwards with a hard strike using the false edge.

---

64 'Pro cum' (in front with) is written above 'in' (in/on). By replacing 'in' with 'pro cum', the meaning of 'Nam mea membra tego validis erectus in armis' would change from 'for I hold my limbs raised in strong armor' to 'for I hold my limbs raised in front with strong armor.' Unlike the other annotations, which seem to facilitate reading the text, the reader probably wrote this annotation to help him remember in more detail how to perform the action of the paragraph.

65 In the text, the phrase that translates to 'raised in strong armor' is written as 'validis erect' in armis.' The apostrophe at the end of erect' replaces the letter 'a'. The phrase should read 'validis erecta in armis' but when spoken, the final 'a' in 'erecta' would be elided because the next word 'in' begins with a vowel. The author excluded the final 'a' in 'erecta' to show this elision.

66 Here the position is called 'mediana porta ferri' instead of 'ferrea mediana janua.' Both phrases can be translated as 'middle iron door' or 'middle door of iron.'

20r Top

> *This lies exposed in context as the illustration demonstrates as a witness. And here you see because*[67] *I can destroy you with a dagger.*

This image depicts a play from a master not shown in the Paris version of the Flower of Battle. In the Getty the master with the dagger waits for his opponent to thrust or cut. In response the student, (shown as a remedy master in the Paris) passes back, so that the left leg is leading. The sword is deflected to the right, while the student grips the opponent's wrist with his left hand.

From the Getty MS Ludwig XV 13.

20r Bottom

> *Your dagger succeeded in nothing, so quickly have I forced you to turn your back, you will not be able to show me your anguished face.*

The crowned master is shown as a crowned and garter wearing counter-master in the Getty. As a response to the play above, the counter-master grips the opponent's left elbow as they reach for the counter-master's arm. A push to the left turns the opponent, exposing their back, so that the counter-master can thrust with his sword.

---

67 The text shows the letter 'q' Berthaut interprets this as shorthand for 'quod' (because). This interpretation fits the meter and the meaning.

¶ This lies exposed in context as the illustration demonstrates as a witness. And here you see because I can destroy you with a dagger.

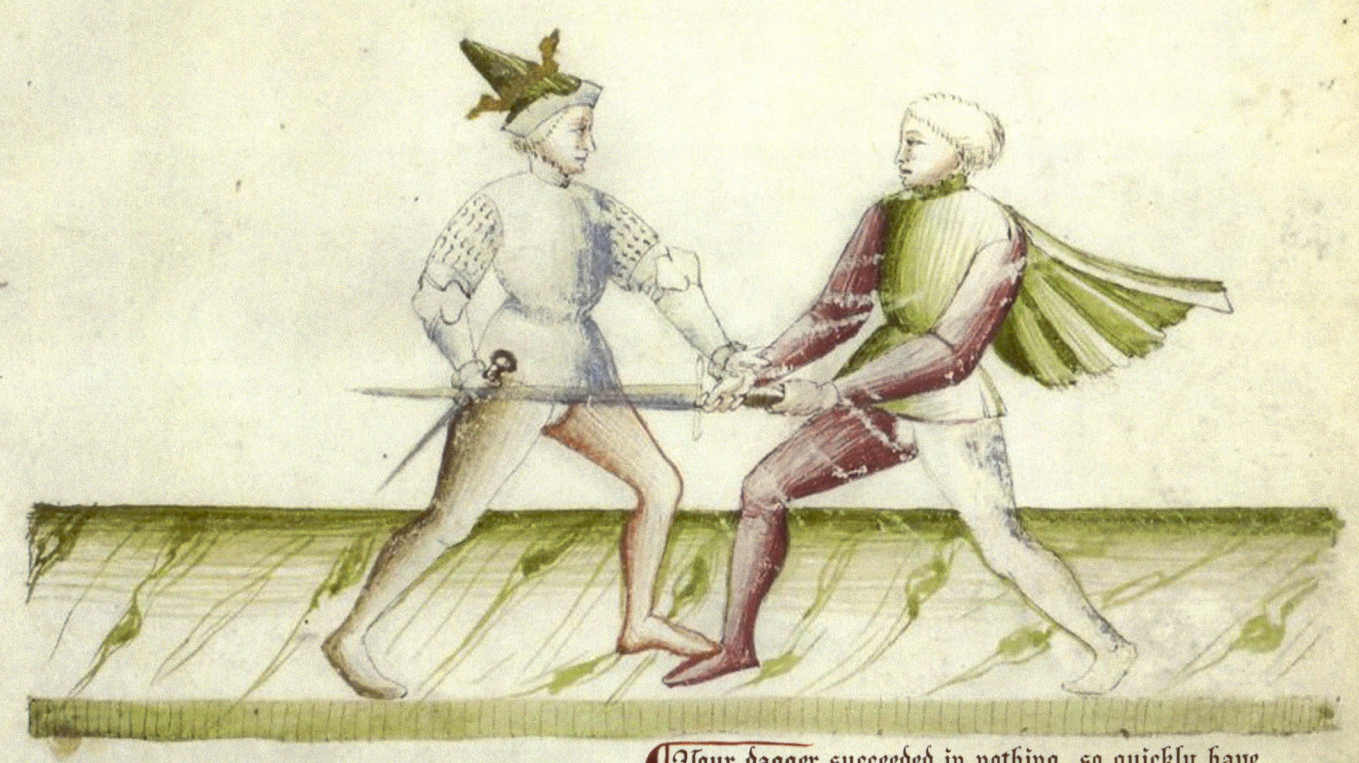

¶ Your dagger succeeded in nothing, so quickly have I forced you to turn your back, you will not be able to show me your anguished face.

If anyone should strike the sword under my head, I would make this guard by grabbing the elbow with my left hand and with my own hand I would turn the back of the one playing from which position I would strike his kidneys by penetrating with the dagger.

This is the best movement of the play in the art and it is guarded, and I will not cover and I will strike at the same time by baring the blade.

20v:

20v Top

> *If anyone should strike the sword[68] under[69] my head, I would make this guard by grabbing the elbow with my left hand and with my own hand I would turn the back of the one playing from which position I would strike his kidneys by penetrating with the dagger.[70]*

The student wearing a garter is armed with a dagger. The opponent strikes one-handed with a sword and the student passes forward intercepting the strike. He will be right foot forward at this point and use his left hand to grip the opponent by the elbow and spin him to the right. He can then deliver strikes to the back of the opponent.

20v Bottom

> *This is the best movement of the play in the art and it is guarded, and I will not cover and I will strike at the same time by baring the blade.*

The master has his sword held with the point on the ground. The Getty manuscript indicates that the sword is supposed to be in a scabbard. When the opponent strikes, the master brings the still sheathed sword up into the attacker's arm to thwart him. The master will then pass back, drawing his sword. His scabbard keeps the arm at bay, while passing back creates the distance he needs to free the sword and attack the opponent.

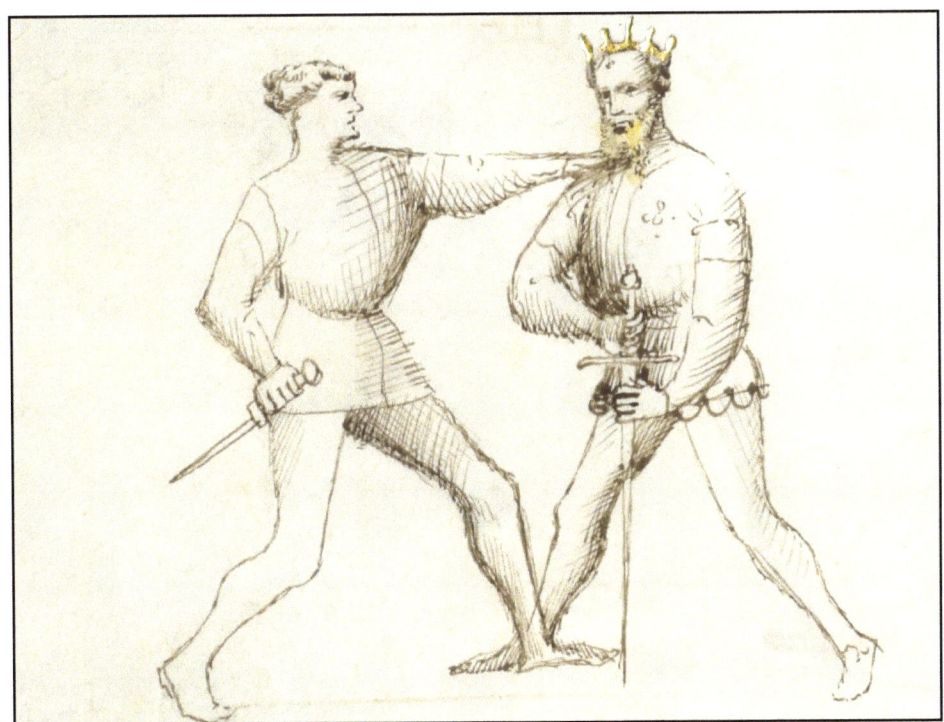

From the Getty MS Ludwig XV 13.

---

68   The word 'spatam' here is different from the usual word for sword in the manuscript, which is 'ensis.' The new word was probably used to fit the meter better. 'Spata' seems to correspond to the Italian word for sword, which is *spada*.

69   The tiny word 'si' (if) above the word 'sub' (under) indicates that this is a conditional statement.

70   Berthaut notes that 'dagam penetrante' seems to replace 'daga penetrando.' The former fits better metrically but the latter makes more sense grammatically. The author probably took liberties with the grammar in order to better fit the meter.

21r

For I will thus bring out a dagger covered by my hand at the sign, I will raise the dagger itself with both hands bearing (it).

Since I defeat all who are capable of warlike things I will be able when I have been equipped with my arms with me instead of injured hands.

By covering my arms[71] to all who are waging war in a circle in such a way that they are unable to hold out a protected right hand[72] I now thus happily bring together two keys in my hands.

You ask why I gloriously ruin such men with my feet, why I say to bring down all men by fighting, indeed my hand pretends to rest on my right side.

This page depicts four crowned masters, each with a bit of wisdom for anyone who fights with the dagger. The Getty more clearly indicates what each master intends. The first holds up a dagger and says to disarm the opponent. The second holds up a pair of arms in the Getty, but holds nothing in the Paris. He tells the reader to dislocate and break the arms of the opponent. The third master holds a key, which symbolizes the upper, middle, and lower locks. The final master, shown as older than the rest, has thrown his opponent to the ground.

The increasing age of the four images are not clearly explained but there are two possible interpretations. First, that is is best to try and disarm, break, lock and throw an opponent. The other, is that each image requires more skill than the last, that it is easier to disarm an opponent than to throw them.

---

71 Here the word used for 'arms' is 'brachia.' Although this technically means 'lower arms' it is sometimes used interchangeably with 'lacerti' (upper arms) to simply mean 'arms.' Fiore probably used 'brachia' because 'lacerti' would not fit the meter. See footnote 73 for more information.
72 In Latin literature, the word 'dextra' (right hand) often refers to the sword itself because it is the sword-hand.

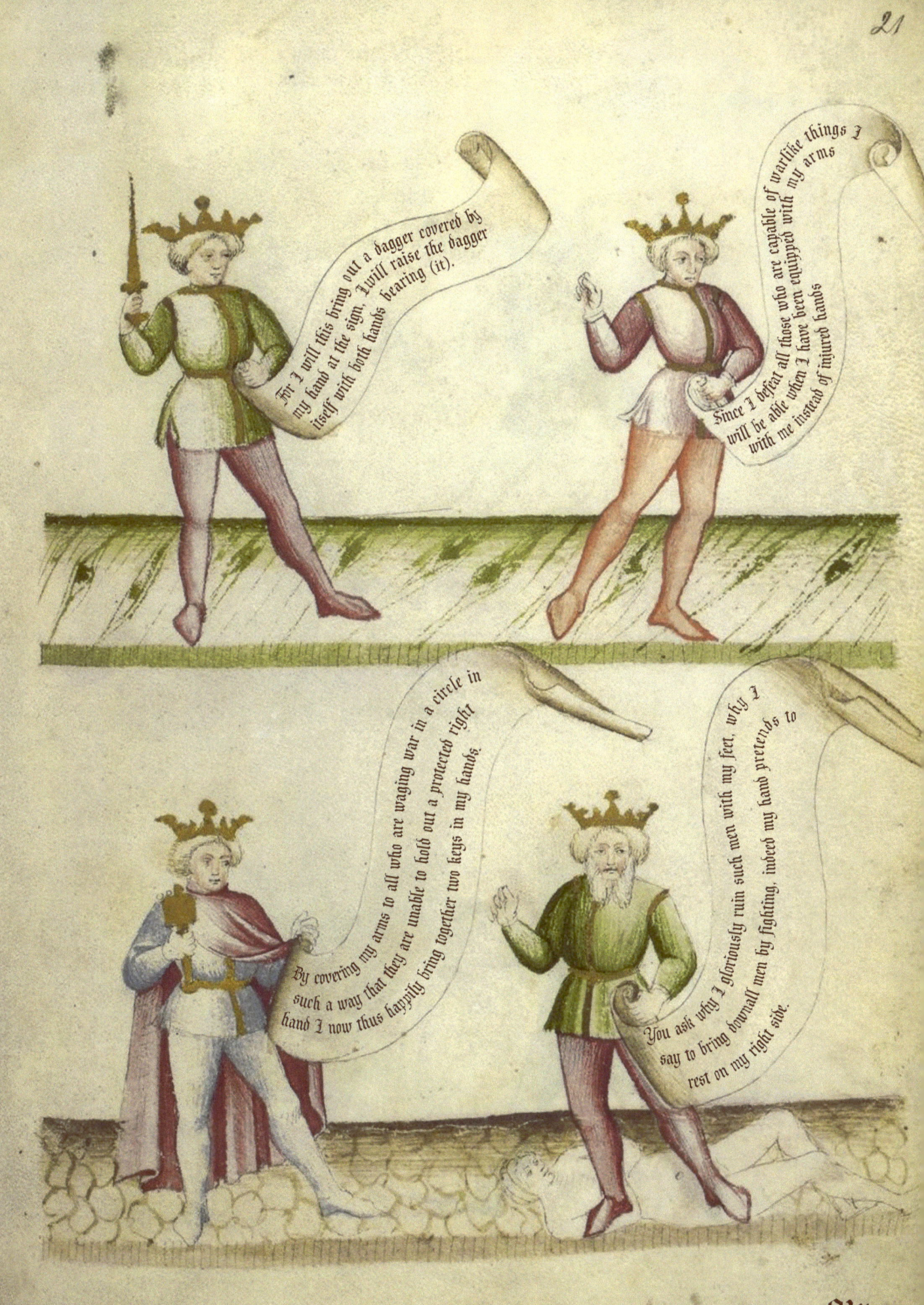

I myself am called the first protected master of the dagger, and I anticipate to raise the dagger with my left hand.

Indeed, I turn the dagger around your arm. By not losing that dagger I will strike you miserably in the chest.

21v:

21v Top

> *I myself am called the first protected master of the dagger, and I anticipate to raise the dagger with my left hand.*

The crowned master is depicted wearing full armor, something he is not in the other versions of the Flower of Battle. The master has waited for his opponent to attack with the dagger and in response has gripped their wrist with his left hand with his thumb pointing down. From here he will twist to the left. His right hand meanwhile is raised and could be used to strike at the opponent, or grip the dagger.

21v Bottom

> *Indeed, I turn the dagger around your arm.[73] By not losing that dagger I will strike you miserably in the chest.*

The crowned and garter wearing counter-master is defeating the prior play. To do this, soon as his wrist is gripped he turns it to the left. This rolls the dagger over the opponent's arm denying them the leverage they needed to complete the play.

From the Getty MS Ludwig XV 13.

---

73 Here the word 'lacertum' (upper arm) is used instead of 'brachium' (lower arm) even though the picture shows the lower-arm being held. This leads me to believe that 'lacertum' and 'bracchium' are used interchangeably to just mean 'arm.' Here at least, the word 'lacertum' fits the meter better than 'bracchium.'

22r Top

Behold, with this opposition your guard is refuted and neither the plays with a turned-around palm nor either the previous plays will succeed. You, miserable man, will then lie down about to die.

The crowned and garter wearing counter-master is defeating the opponent who is trying to use their crossed arms to intercept his attack as seen in 23v bottom. The left hand is used to deceive the defender either by feinting and raising the left arm to invite the opponent to rush in, or by passing the right leg back instantly after the opponent makes the cover, and sliding the left arm under their crossed arms while freeing the dagger.

The play of 23v.

22r Bottom

Indeed, you will treacherously touch the ground now, I believe, and I myself[74] will make worse things for you from here when you are lying down.[75]

The crowned master is defeating an attack that came from the left, instead of an overhand strike from the right. To do this, the master used his right hand to grip the opponent's wrist with the thumb pointing down. A strong pull is given toward his hip while he passes with his left leg behind the opponent. The master's left hand pushes or strikes the opponent's jaw and grips. The grasp to the jaw, the position of the leg and the pull of the right hand allows the master to follow up with various plays.

---

74 'scilicet ego' (certainly I) is written on top of 'ipse' (I myself). See footnote 50.
75 The use of the verb 'credo' (I trust, I believe) at the beginning of the passage should introduce an indirect statement but the preceding words are not structured like an indirect statement so I took the verb 'credo' to be almost an aside rather than an integral part of the sentence.

Behold, with this opposition your guard is refuted and neither the plays with a turned-around palm nor either the previous plays will succeed. You, miserable man, will then lie down about to die.

Indeed, you will treacherously touch the ground now, I believe, and I myself will make worse things for you from here when you are lying down.

¶ You will touch the ground unguarded with your chest lain low. An armored man will be able to approach this play more securely.

¶ As I hold it, anyone could break an arm while his partner is fighting, anyone who will be allowed can feel this.

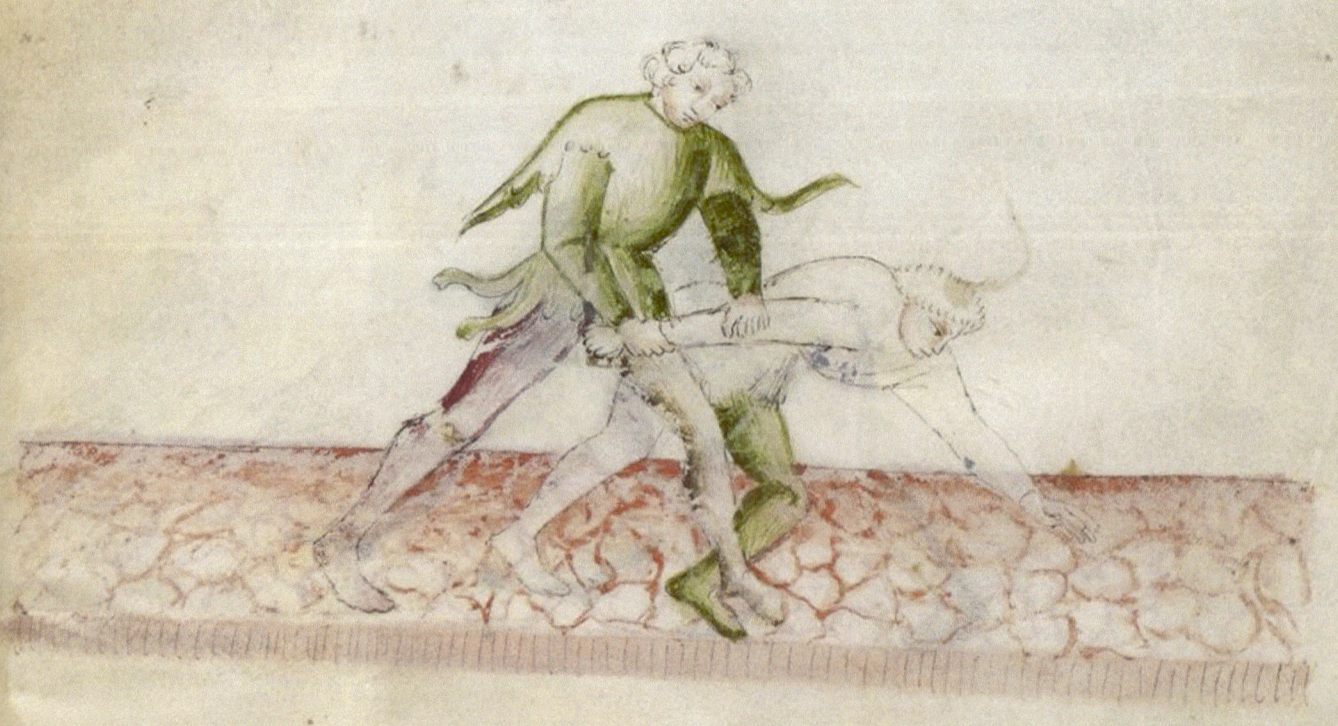

22v Top

You will touch the ground unguarded with your chest lain low. An armored man will be able to approach this play more securely.

The garter wearing student is following up from the prior play. He has released the opponent's hand and has brought his right arm around his opponent's neck, clasping it with his left hand. He can throw the opponent by sharply turning his hips to the left. The other versions of the Flower of Battle suggest that this play is best performed in armor, likely because the dagger has not been controlled.

22v Bottom

As I hold it, anyone could break an arm while his partner is fighting, anyone who will be allowed can feel this.[76]

The garter wearing student is performing another follow up from the play of 22r bottom. He has placed his left foot in front of the opponent's legs, while using his left arm to push onto the opponent's elbow so as to break it. The right hand continues to grip the opponent's wrist. This play works best if the opponent's arm is straight, making a lock difficult, but a break easier.

The play of 22r.

---

76 A more literal translation of this phrase would be 'it is given to feel to anyone to whom it will be permitted.'

23r:

23r Top

> *Because of the disarm which this master now performs, you will not leave without a broken arm,[77] I trust.[78]*

The garter wearing student is performing a follow up play from 21v top. He has intercepted the dagger strike and has passed under the arm of the opponent. He is using both of his hands to break the opponent's arm over his left shoulder. To do this, the opponent's arm needs to be twisted so that the elbow is leveraged the wrong direction. A downward pull breaks the arm.

23r Bottom

> *I will suddenly snatch the dagger with a violent twist, nevertheless I will strongly twist the lower-arm[79] a little bit in front of the elbow.*

The garter wearing student is performing a follow up play from 21v top. He has intercepted the dagger strike and is using his left hand to grab the dagger. To disarm the opponent the student pushes the point of the dagger toward the opponent's elbow. This puts pressure on where the opponent's grip is the weakest at the thumb.

The remedy master of 21v.

---

77 A more literal translation of this would be 'without a break of the arm.'
78 See footnote 75 for the way the verb 'credo' (I trust) is used here.
79 In this case, the word 'brachia' seems to refer to the lower-arm and does not just mean 'arm.' See footnote 71 and 73.

Because of the disarm which this master now performs, you will not leave without a broken arm, I trust.

I will suddenly snatch the dagger with a violent twist, nevertheless I will strongly twist the lower-arm a little bit in front of the elbow.

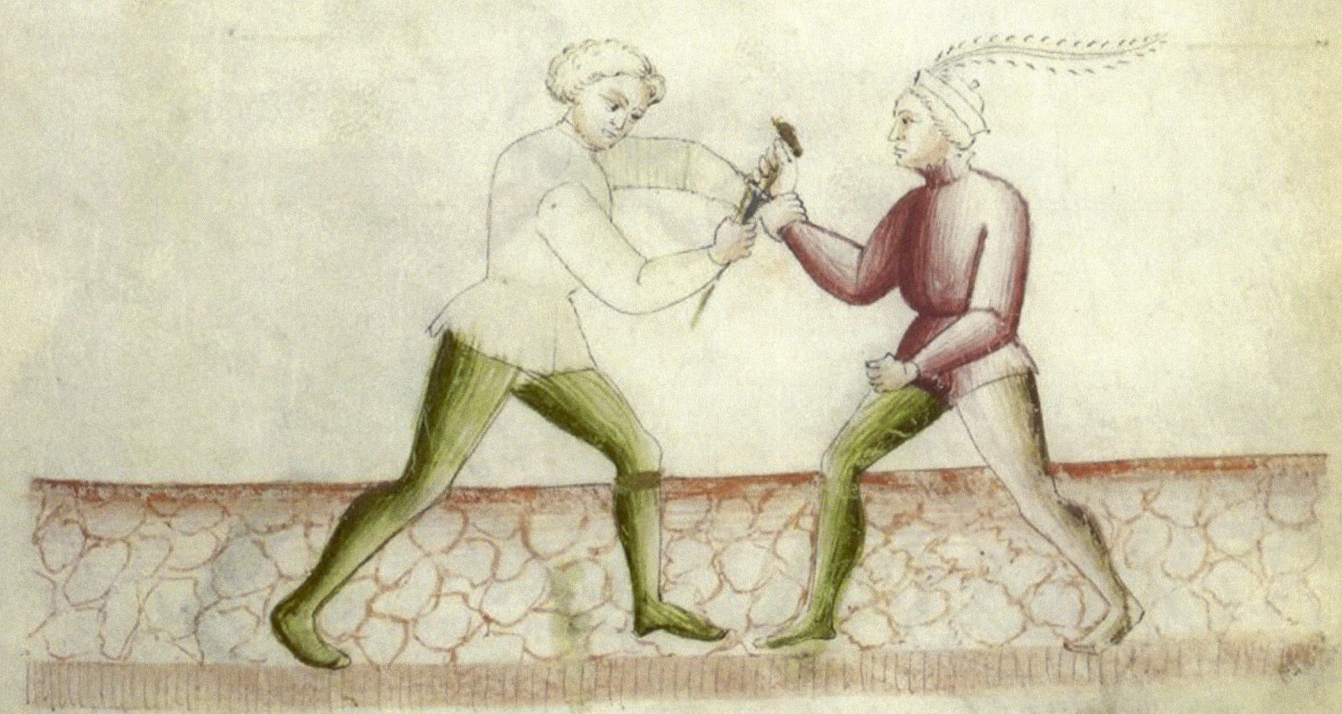

¶ It takes no effort for me to lay you low while you are falling,
You will not be able to get up freely without a large wound.

¶ Thus, I cover myself with my arms while fighting in the
bind, and I can contend with all the first methods.

23v Top

> *It takes no effort for me to lay you low while you are falling, you will not be able to get up freely without a large wound.*

The garter wearing student is performing a follow up play from 21v top. After intercepting the opponent's wrist, the student has placed his left leg to the outside of the opponent's legs. His left hand remains clasped to the opponent's wrist, while his right arm hooks around the right leg of the opponent. From here the opponent can be thrown and if the opponent is too heavy, or is attempting to squat and so increase their stability, the student can drive his shoulder into the opponent's hips.

The remedy master of 21v.

23v Bottom

> *Thus, I cover myself with my arms while fighting in the bind, and I can contend with all the first methods.*

The garter wearing student is depicted as a master in the Getty. The student has passed forward and rather than use his left hand to grab the opponent's wrist, he has instead crossed his arms and driven into the opponent's attack. In the Getty, and in 25v top, the cover is made to the outside of the dagger. This play uses a common strategy in Fiore's art to use two hands to counter strength. If the opponent was much larger, for example, one hand might not stop the incoming strike. The counter to this play is shown in 22r top.

The Getty and 25v play on the outside of the opponent's dagger.

22r, the counter play.

24r Top

Look, your right hand is enclosed by my left arm, many bad things hinder you when you are restrained.

The garter wearing student is performing a follow up play from 21v top. After intercepting the opponent's wrist, or perhaps missing the grip and extending their hand too far, the left arm is used to slip over the opponent's right arm. The student steps with his left leg behind the opponent's right leg. This is the middle lock and by using his chest to compress the opponent's arm and pointing upwards with the left hand, the opponent's elbow is bent. The picture shows the opponent has been disarmed and the dagger is safely under the foot of the student.

The remedy master of 21v.

24r Bottom

It is not permitted for you to hold the compressed arm by holding back nevertheless the pressure will hurt you from the lower key.

The crowned and garter wearing counter-master is defeating the prior play. As the opponent attempts the middle lock, the counter-master has brought his left hand in to grip his right wrist. The two arms of the counter-master thwart the one of the opponent. From here the dagger can be driven into the opponent, his arm can be broken or he can be thrown.

Look, your right hand is enclosed by my left arm, many bad things hinder you when you are restrained.

It is not permitted for you to hold the compressed arm by holding back nevertheless the pressure will hurt you from the lower key.

¶ If I myself am able to twist your arm with my hands now you will always remain miserably in the middle key.

¶ You will not make me spend time in the middle key, but with this opposition it now brings me to you in order that you yield to me.

24v Top

If I myself am able to twist your arm with my hands now you will always remain miserably in the middle key.

The garter wearing student is performing a follow up play from 21v top. After intercepting the opponent's wrist the student has stepped on the opponent's right foot with his left foot, while pushing down and to the left with his right hand. The student's left hand is used to grab the opponent's elbow and lift up and to the right. The two hands are used to bend the arm, so that the middle lock can be then performed, or the right hand can grip the opponent behind the right knee.

21v and potential follow up actions from 24v, including the middle lock or a grab of the leg.

24v Bottom

You will not make me spend time in the middle key, but with this opposition it now brings me to you in order that you yield to me.

The crowned and garter wearing counter-master is defeating the prior technique. As the opponent grips his wrist and elbow, the counter-master uses his left hand to grip his own dagger. The opponent will not be able to overpower the counter-master who can drive the point of his dagger into the opponent forcing them to let go.

25r Top

> Now I can[80] push you onto the ground because you have been cut down, and if the opposition is lacking, I will do it to you when you have been pressed.

The garter wearing student is performing a follow up play from 21v top. After intercepting the opponent's wrist, the student has slid his right arm forward to put the opponent in the upper lock. By looking at the Getty and Pisani-Dossi versions of the Flower of Battle a progression of the lock can be made out. From the initial move, as seen in the Paris, to the left arm moving over the opponent's right, as seen in the Getty, and finally to the left hand gripping the right wrist as seen in the Pisani-Dossi. From this lock it is possible to throw the opponent to the ground by placing the right leg behind the opponent's right leg and driving forward while maintaining the lock.

The remedy master of 21v.

25r Bottom

> Now I hasten this opposition just as you will duly see, from there I will strike your limbs with a burning spirit.

The crowned and garter wearing counter-master is defeating the prior technique. As the opponent attempts the upper lock, the counter-master uses his left hand to grab behind his right wrist. This provides more strength to both drive the dagger into the opponent and prevent them from getting the leverage necessary to complete the upper lock.

---

80   Here the author uses 'Aptus sum' rather than the more common 'possum' to mean 'I can.' This is necessary to fit the meter.

¶ Now I can push you onto the ground because you have been cut down, and if the opposition is lacking, I will do it to you when you have been pressed.

¶ Now I hasten this opposition just as you will duly see, from there I will strike your limbs with a burning spirit.

⁋ I cover myself as you see because I have been moved by great strength, I attempt the methods which anyone before was able to perform.

⁋ Now with this opposition I deceive the previous plays, and I will twist in such a way because afterwards I will destroy you with a wound.

25v Top

I cover myself as you see because I have been moved by great strength, I attempt the methods which anyone before was able to perform.

This play is similar to 23v bottom. The student has gripped his own wrist to intercept the opponent's attack and come to the outside of the opponent's attack. The use of two hands increases strength and could be used to stop a powerful blow. From here a variety of plays are possible including those from the strikes from the left as seen in 22r bottom.

23v, a similar play and 22r, a remedy master who defeats attacks from the left.

25v Bottom

Now with this opposition I deceive the previous plays, and I will twist in such a way because afterwards I will destroy[81] you with a wound.

The crowned and garter wearing counter-master is defeating the prior play. This counter is performed by the counter-master gripping the opponent's right elbow and pushing upwards to turn them and expose their back.

---

81 Berthaut says that 'id est occidam' (that is, I will kill you) is written above the word 'perdam' (I will destroy). I could only make out the word 'occidam' (I will kill).

26r Top

Indeed, I will cut off your face so quickly with this action, the student teaches this when he leads the fold of the sword through the ground from this cross, but your blade will leave either bent or broken; you will never be able to use it.[82]

The garter wearing student has defeated a thrust by having his left foot move to the left, then passing with the right and striking a fendente into the middle of the opponent's blade. From here, the student has stepped upon the opponent's sword and is delivering a false edge cut. This is similar to the play from 15v bottom.

The play of 15v.

26r Bottom

I will strike and I will hold your blade with no defense stopping me, so poorly do you yourself control my blade while holding the bind.[83] *Now you will die when you have been pierced by my blade.*

The garter wearing student is reacting from a close bind. The student has passed his left leg forward and gripped the opponent's wrist. This can be done either moving over or under the crossing of the blades. From here the student can retract his sword to thrust or cut. The play is similar to the one seen in 15r bottom.

The play of 15r.

---

82 ''pro operari' (to work at it in front) is written below 'operarier' (to use). This is probably another of the text-owner's annotations.

83 Here the word 'iura,' a form of 'ius, iuris (n.)' (right), is used to mean 'bind' because rights are binding and 'that which binds' is a secondary definition of 'ius, iuris'.

¶ Indeed, I will cut off your face so quickly with this action, the student teaches this when he leads the fold of the sword through the ground from this cross, but your blade will leave either bent or broken; you will never be able to use it.

¶ I will strike and I will hold your blade with no defense stopping me, so poorly do you yourself control my blade while holding the bind. Now you will die when you have been pierced by my blade.

With this pommel, I strike your face as you are indeed aggressive. This is because you have struck the sword with the deepest touches.

This is another blow to strike back at your partner with the pommel provided that nevertheless this art and the master himself are fast.

26v:

26v Top

> *With this pommel, I strike your face as you are indeed aggressive. This is because you have struck the sword with the deepest touches.*

The garter wearing student is reacting from a close bind. He has passed forward to the outside of the opponent's right foot while grabbing his opponent's right arm with his left hand. He has driven the pommel into the opponent's face.

26v Bottom

> *This is another blow to strike back at your partner[84] with the pommel provided that nevertheless this art and the master himself are fast.*

The garter wearing student is performing a similar play to the prior. From the close bind he has passed forward allowing the opponent's blade to slide off of his while he delivers a two-handed pommel strike to the opponent's head. Fiore notes in the Getty version that this strike has enough power to defeat even an armored opponent and knock out teeth. Four of them to be exact. The Getty also depicts the sword to the student's left side which can be achieved by raising the hands high over the head when ceding the opponent's sword and then driving the pommel into the face.

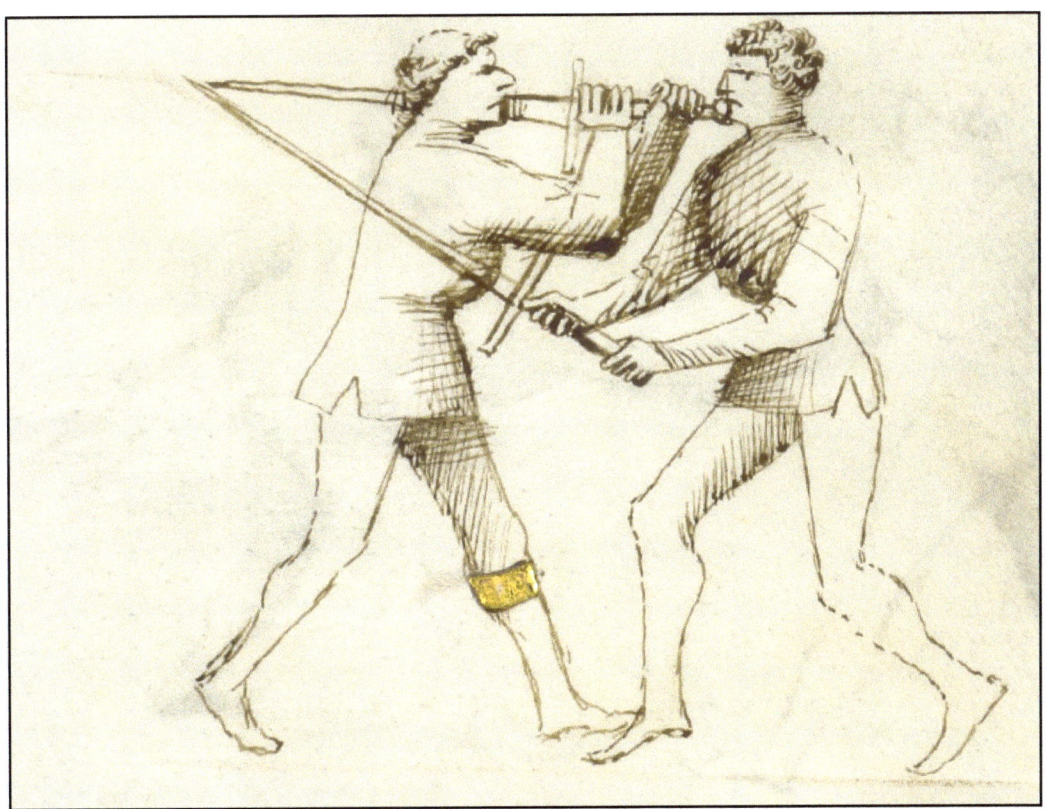

From the Getty MS Ludwig XV 13.

---

84   Here the word 'sodalez' is used for partner, which is used on 33V and 36R. The word 'socius' is used for 'partner' on 22V, 31R, 32R, 32V, 43V.

27r:

27r Top

In the bind, I very forcefully snatch your very own sword, or I will strike you with the point here when you have been cut down with a cut, I am said to raise my hands opposite to the sword,[85] and I can openly strike your limbs, you will not be able to touch the sword with any injuries.[86]

The garter wearing student is reacting from a close bind. He has passed back, reaching under the opponent's sword to grasp their quillion. This traps the blade in the student's arm, while his sword is free to strike.

27r Bottom

I throw you onto the ground with a large action which you perceive, I have not been deceived to place the sword on your neck.

This play shows a possible play to perform after completing the pommel strike from 26v bottom. After hitting the opponent the garter wearing student has passed so their right leg is leading and thrown their sword and arm around the opponent's neck. If the opponent has no armor there, their throat can be cut or the student can attempt a throw.

The play of 26v.

---

85   Here the word 'spata' (sword) is used again instead of the more common 'ensis' (sword). This seems to be for metrical reasons. See footnote 68 and 89.
86   The word for injuries here is 'violatibus' which must be an alternate form of the word 'violationibus.'

¶ In the bind, I very forcefully snatch your very own sword, or I will strike you with the point here when you have been cut down with a cut, I am said to raise my hands opposite to the sword, and I can openly strike your limbs, you will not be able to touch the sword with any injuries.

¶ I throw you onto the ground with a large action which you perceive, I have not been deceived to place the sword on your neck.

❡ I learn to strike back at your own upper-arms with your sword, I will either strike you or at the same time as this I will enclose your lower arms.

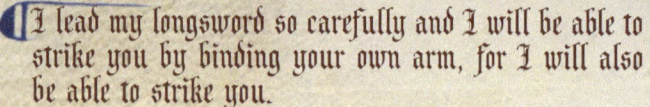

❡ I lead my longsword so carefully and I will be able to strike you by binding your own arm, for I will also be able to strike you.

27v Top

> *I learn to strike back at your own upper-arms with your sword, I will either strike you or at the same time as this[87] I will enclose your lower arms.[88]*

The garter wearing student is reacting from a close bind. The student has passed forward and slid their left hand between the opponent's hands so as to grab their right forearm. From here, the wrist is twisted to the left in a way similar to the dagger play of 21v top. Even if the play is not immediately successful, the left hand can disrupt the opponent long enough for the student to get his sword free and attack.

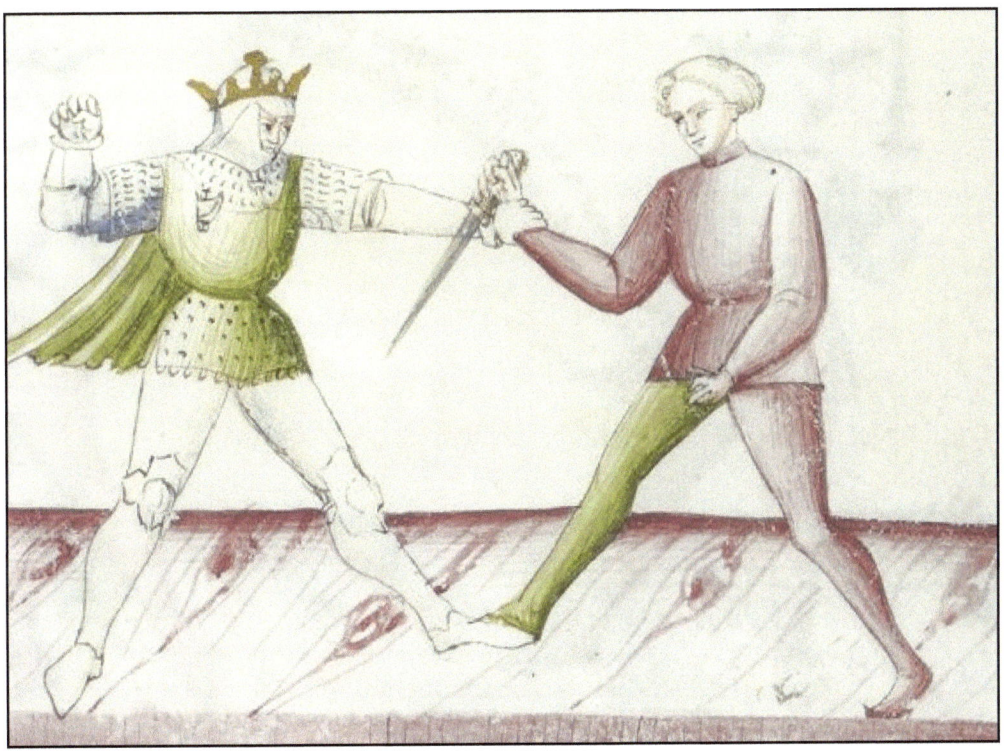

The remedy master of 21v.

27v Bottom

> *I lead my longsword so carefully and I will be able to strike you by binding your own arm, for I will also be able to strike you.*

The garter wearing student is reacting from a close bind. This play can progress from the one above. The student has passed with his left leg to the inside of the opponent while wrapping his left arm around the opponent's right arm.

---

87 'tum' (then) is written above 'hoc' (this) (Berthaut).

88 In most of the text, the words 'lacertus' (upper arm) and 'brachium' (lower arm) are used interchangeably to mean 'arm.' However, on 27V, both words occur so we can assume 'lacertus' refers to the upper arm and 'brachia' refers to the lower arms. See footnote 71 and 73 for more information.

28r:

28r Top

You have come in order that you might be able to take away the sword[89] with the left hand,[90] in the end, you yourself will perish in the opposite way here.

This garter wearing student should have a crown and be a counter-master. He is countering the play from 27v top by passing back and bringing his right hand to his own sword. In this way he has created distance and given himself more strength to oppose the opponent's grip.

The play of 27v (top).

28r Bottom

You wanted to enclose the sword under your own arm falsely but this will also turn you all the way around.[91]

This garter wearing and crowned counter-master is defeating the play from 27v bottom. As the opponent attempts to wrap up the counter-master's right arm, the counter-master has gripped his own sword with his left hand and pulled down and to the left. This places the opponent into the lower lock.

The play of 27v (bottom).

---

89   Here the word 'ensis' (sword) is used instead of the word 'spata' (sword). Once again, this seems to be a product of the meter. See footnote 68 and 85.

90   There is a cross between convellere (to grab) and contrario (in the opposite way) (Berthaut).

91   The word 'nexio' is used to mean 'bind' instead of 'nexura,' which was used in 16V, 17V, 31V, 37R, 38R, and 44R.

¶ You have come in order that you might be able to take away the sword with the left hand, in the end, you yourself will perish in the opposite way here.

¶ You wanted to enclose the sword under your own arm falsely but this will also turn you all the way around.

¶ I have enclosed your hand with my sword, you at last will wretchedly suffer many wounds from the point and whatever I myself perform, I do it against the blade, and this bind is very powerful because it administers many deeds.

¶ I have gone under into the oblique part from the upright side, therefore you will depart from your miserable life with this point.

28v Top

> *I have enclosed your hand with my sword, you at last will wretchedly suffer many wounds from the point[92] and whatever I myself perform, I do it against the blade, and this bind[93] is very powerful because it administers many deeds.[94]*

This play is better depicted in the Novati where the victor is shown as a counter-master to close plays. The counter-master has passed in and grasped the right wrist of his opponent. He can then deliver thrusts. In the Paris, the play depicts a master who is right leg leading and in the process of reaching for the opponent's wrist or forearm.

From the Novati Pisani-Dossi.

28v Bottom

> *I have gone under into the oblique part from the upright side, therefore you will depart from your miserable life with this point.*

The garter wearing student is reacting from a close bind. He has passed forward, placing his left leg behind the opponent while gripping his own sword with his left hand and driving it into the opponent's chest. This play may also be from the Getty's depiction of the false point, where a feint is thrown to the opponent's right, and after they cover, the student passes and goes to the half sword.

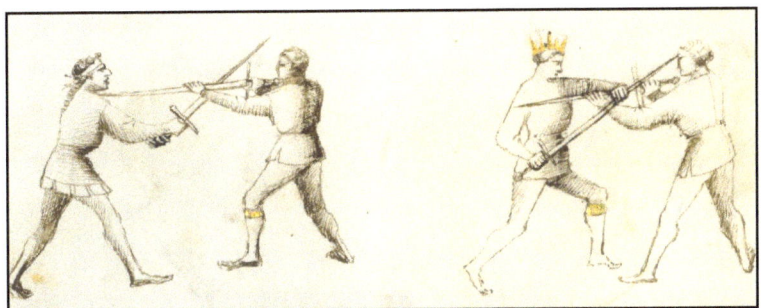

The play and counter of the false point from the Getty MS Ludwig XV 13.

---

92   Here the word 'vertice' is used for point instead of 'cuspide,' which was used in 3R, 3V, 4V, 6V, 8V, 10R, 10V, 11V, 12V, 13R, 13V, 14R, 15R, 17R, 18R, 18V, 19V, 27R, 28V, and 31R. Either choice would fit the meter though.

93   Here the word 'Nexio' is used for 'bind' instead of the usual word 'nexura,' which would not fit the meter.

94   'It does many things.'

29r Top

This movement in the play by which I deprive a man of his blade is called by everyone in weaponry the high right, which I myself, Florius, have demonstrated in many different ways.

The garter wearing student is reacting from a close bind. The student is attempting to disarm the opponent. The Paris' depiction is different than the others. In the Getty, for example, the student has his left arm wrapped around the opponent's blade and his hilt is on the outside of the blade as well. From here, by moving both hands clockwise the high disarm is completed. The Paris depicts the disarm with the grip and hilt on the inside and so there is no easy way to perform the technique and this may be an artistic error.

From the Getty MS Ludwig XV 13.

29r Bottom

By receiving the middle of the sword, I straight away engage a strike by pushing your limbs with either my own furious blade or perhaps your blade which you trust is present.

The garter wearing student is performing a disarm from the close bind. The student's left hand has moved between the opponent's hands, while the hilt of his blade is pressed to the outside of the opponent's sword. From here, both hands move clockwise to perform the middle disarm.

¶ This movement in the play by which I deprive a man of his blade is called by everyone in weaponry the high right, which I myself, Florius, have demonstrated in many different ways.

¶ By receiving the middle of the sword, I straight away engage a strike by pushing your limbs with either my own furious blade or perhaps your blade which you trust is present.

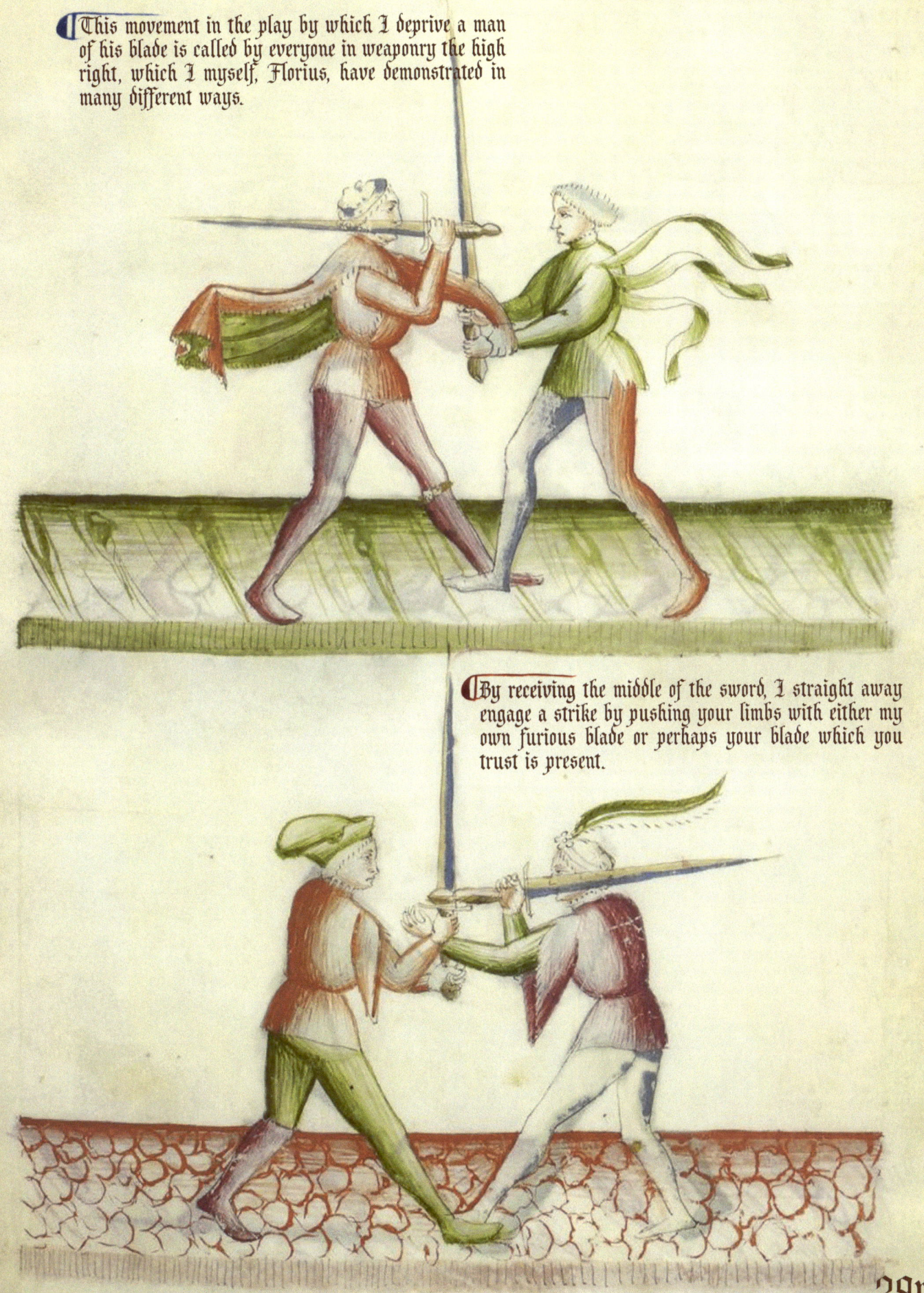

❡ In this way the sharp sword is captured in the lower place, which anyone who remains experienced in this art may do.

❡ I consider that it is indeed my blade which you perceive, and by twisting I will certainly make shame for you, and I will drag it back with my own hands if the fates do not resist.

29v Top

In this way the sharp sword is captured in the lower place, which anyone who remains experienced in this art may do.[95]

The garter wearing student is performing a disarm from the close bind. The student's left hand has gripped the pommel of the opponent's sword. The student's hilt is to the outside of the opponent's sword. From here, both hands move clockwise to perform the lower disarm.

29v Bottom

I consider that it is indeed my blade which you perceive, and by twisting I will certainly make shame for you, and I will drag it back with my own hands if the fates do not resist.

The garter wearing student is performing a disarm from the close bind. The student has dropped his sword and gripped the opponent's pommel with his left hand and the opponent's blade with his right hand. From here, both hands move clockwise to perform the final disarm. Passing back and twisting the hips hard can lend strength to any of the disarms.

The play of 29v is identical in nature to the play from 10r.

---

95 There is a cross between 'ensis' (sword) and 'manet' (remains).

30r Top

The further right guard warns in order that I may hold you by the throat, you then miserably may be spread onto the dark ground.

The garter wearing student has covered from an attack on his right side. From here he passes forward placing his right leg behind the opponent's right leg while throwing his sword and arm around the opponent's neck. The student grabs his own sword and can throw the opponent by twisting to the left and pulling their sword down and to the left.

30r Bottom

With a similar play, I spread you onto the low ground, I will also complete this, nevertheless I myself[96] will remain on my feet.

The garter wearing student is performing a similar play to the prior one. If the opponent throws a left to right strike, the student does the same intercepting the opponent's attack and pushing it to the right while passing. From here the play is identical to the prior one.

---

[96] 'ego' (I) is written above 'ipse' (I myself). See footnote 50.

The further right guard warns in order that I may hold you by the throat, you then miserably may be spread onto the dark ground.

With a similar play, I spread you onto the low ground, I will also complete this, nevertheless I myself will remain on my feet.

¶ I accept the disarm that has been discussed for a long time with my hands in order that I may be able to lay you miserably on the ground.

¶ You will go splayed on your back onto the ground and my sword will hold your face. The defense of the strong right arm has demonstrated this.

30v:

30v Top

I accept the disarm that has been discussed for a long time with my hands in order that I may be able to lay you miserably on the ground.

The garter wearing student is reacting to a play depicted in the Getty version. If the opponent covers on their right side, the student uses his left hand to grab the tip of the opponent's sword. From here, the student abandons his sword and passes so his right leg is behind the opponent and his right hand grabs the opponent's hilt. The grasped sword allows the student to cut his opponent's face, or throw him by twisting hard to the left.

From the Getty MS Ludwig XV 13.

30v Bottom

You will go[97] splayed on your back onto the ground and my sword will hold your face. The defense of the strong right arm has demonstrated this.

The garter wearing student has covered on their right side. Instantly after, he has passed forward with his right leg and slid his right hand under the armpit of the opponent's right arm. The left arm has drawn back. The student has grasped his own sword and with a sharp twist to the left can throw his opponent.

---

97 There is a cross written above 'ibis' (you will go) (Berthaut).

31r Top

Anyone could tie down the arm for his partner and to condemn him to death with the point of his own[98] dagger.

The garter wearing student is performing a follow up play from 22r bottom, a left to right strike with the dagger. After preventing the strike, the student has placed his left foot in front of the opponent while his left arm presses hard on their elbow. At the same time, the student pulls his right arm up and can twist hard to the right to dislocate the opponent's arm.

31r Bottom

Now I snatch your dagger, I cannot deceive, and if I want I will be able to bind you on the neck when you are turned.[99]

The garter wearing student is performing a follow up play from a left to right strike with the dagger. After preventing the strike, the student has placed their left foot in front of the opponent while sharply turning to the right. The student's left hand seeks to pull the opponent's dagger free by guiding its tip toward the opponent's thumb, where their grip is weakest.

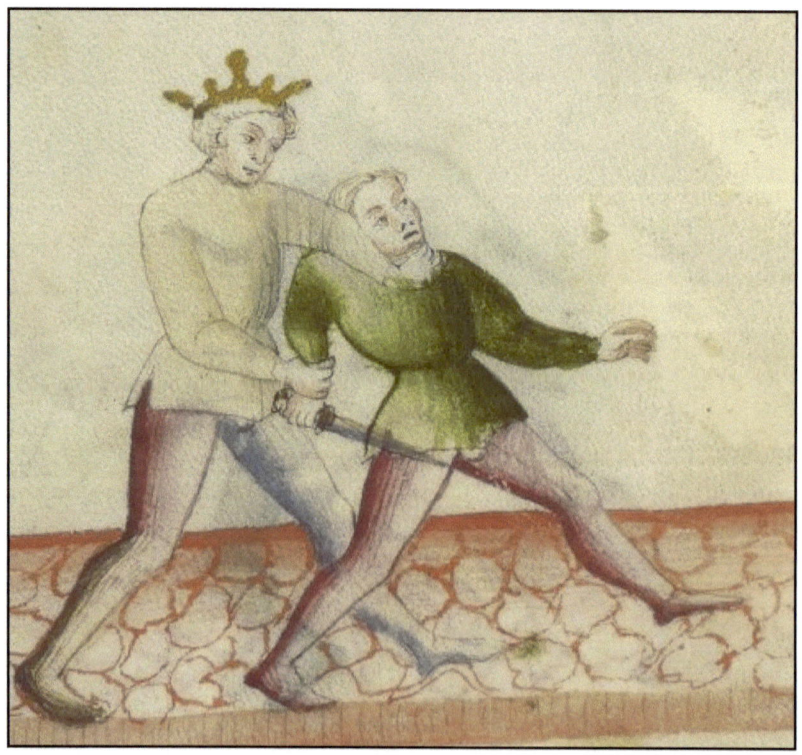

The remedy master of 22r.

---

98   The reflexive-possessive adjective 'sua' (his own) should refer to the subject of the sentence (in this case, the man twisting the other man's arm) but since the dagger in question belongs to the man being twisted, it seems like it refers to him.

99   'id est revolutum' (that is turned back) is written above 'versum' (turned) (Berthaut). Once again, the manuscript owner annotated the text for himself.

¶ Anyone could tie down the arm for his partner and to condemn him to death with the point of his own dagger.

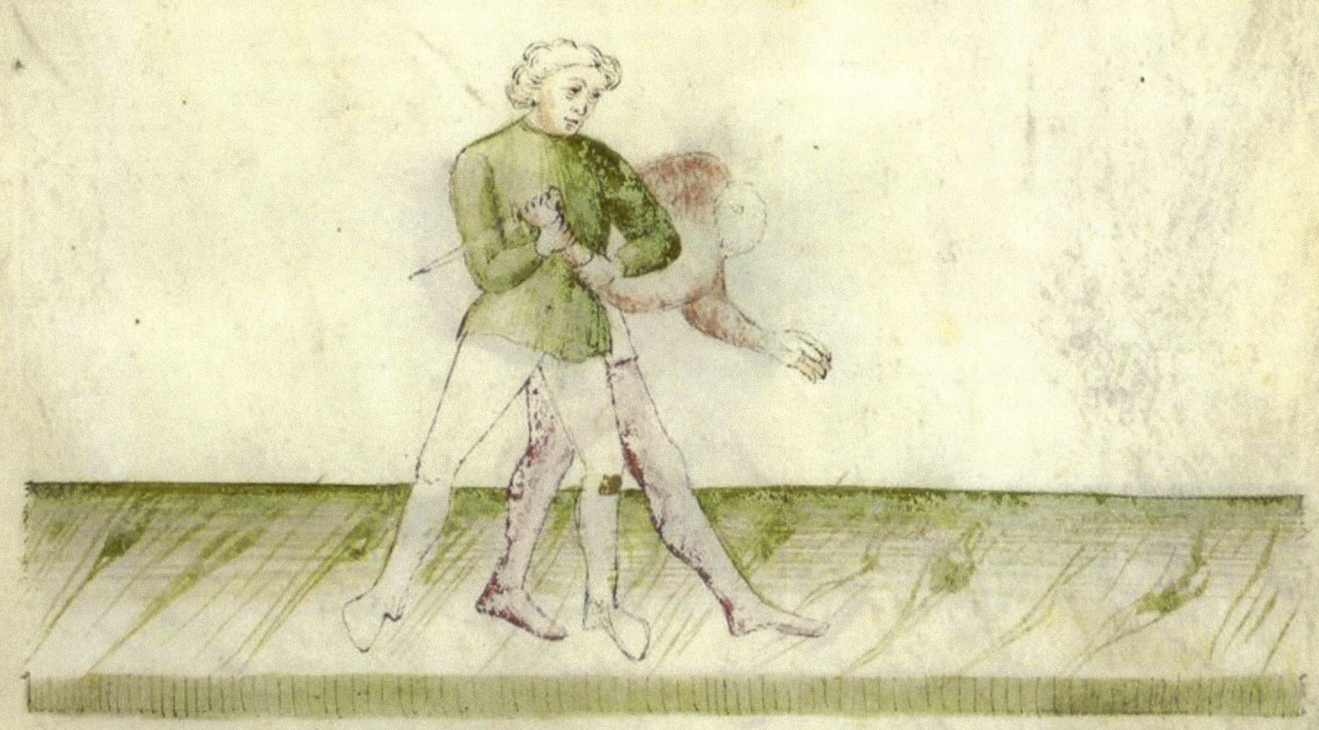

¶ Now I snatch your dagger, I cannot deceive, and if I want I will be able to bind you on the neck when you are turned.

¶ The lower key is carried under its name. It is indeed a strong bind with too great a risk of death. If anyone should enter into this he will scarcely be able to exit from it.

¶ I accomplish this counter-play to the master's play effecting it with either palm of the hands turned around, and you will fall forwards with your knee bent from this disarm.

31v Top

The lower key is carried under its name. It is indeed a strong bind with too great a risk of death.[100] *If anyone should enter into this he will scarcely be able to exit from it.*

The garter wearing student is performing a follow up play from a left to right strike with the dagger. After preventing the strike, the student has placed their left foot in front the opponent. The left hand then releases the opponent's wrist and slipped under their arm, reaching for the opponent's triceps. The student has finally passed back. Their left arm has put the opponent in the lower lock, while their right arm is free to seek a disarm or strike.

31v Bottom

I accomplish this counter-play to the master's play effecting it with either palm of the hands turned around, and you will fall forwards with your knee bent from this disarm.

The garter wearing and crowned counter-master is thwarting the technique from 21v top. After the opponent has made the catch to the wrist, the counter-master has passed back and reached under his own wrist to grab his dagger, so as to put the opponent's hand in a vice between the dagger and the crossed arms. By twisting hard and to the left the opponent can be made to offer up their back, allowing the counter-mater to strike. The technique also works to counter a strike from left to right as seen in 22r bottom.

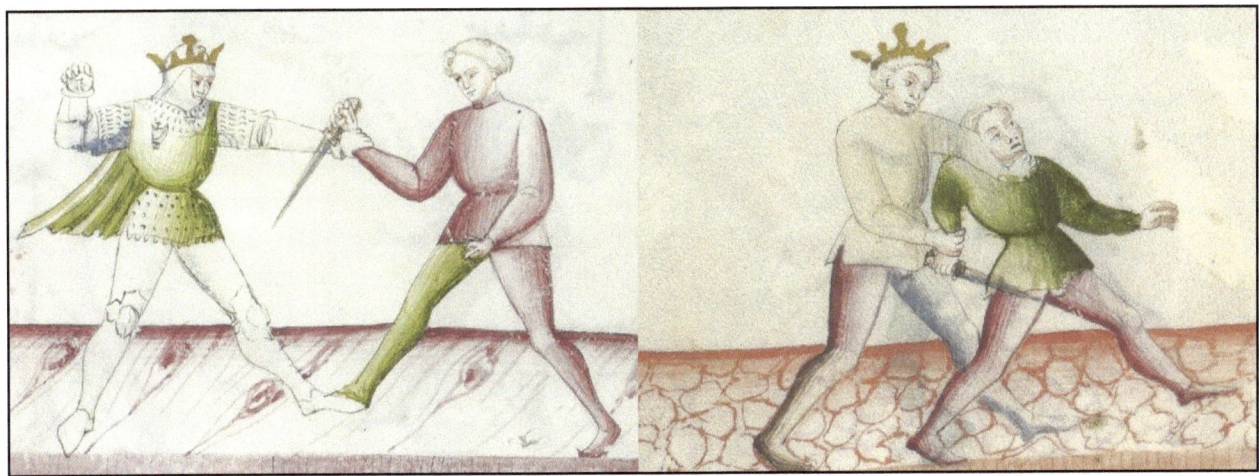

The remedy masters of 21v and 22r.

---

100 Considering that Fiore's plays are all intended to be lethal, the comment that the bind is 'nimio discrimine mortis' (with too great a risk of death) seems like praise of this technique rather than a warning.

32r:

32r Top

> *Now I the master[101] grab my partner with both hands, I can strike you with the iron[102] both from above and from below.*

The crowned master is preventing an overhand strike from above, rather than one from the right or left. His right hand has gripped the opponent's wrist with his thumb up and the left hand has gripped just beneath, also with the thumb up.

32r Bottom

> *I am indeed prepared to send you down onto the ground,[103] and I will give many bad things to your head if I feel like it.[104]*

After stopping the dagger attack from above, the garter wearing student moves into an upper lock. The Getty depicts the left leg farther away, and the Pisani-Dossi shows the student passing with his right leg behind the opponent. The Paris shows the left leg in front of the opponent, making the follow up pass difficult and indicating a possible error. The student's right arm is to the outside of the opponent's. Once the right leg is behind the opponent and the right arm is to the outside of the opponent's arm, a sharp twist to the left can dislocate the opponent's arm.

From the Getty and Novati.

---

101 'ego scilicet' (I of course) is written above 'magister' (master) (Berthaut).
102 'ferro' (iron or sword/dagger) is used here instead of the previous word 'daga' (dagger) to fit the meter.
103 A more literal translation would be 'I have indeed been prepared in order that I may send you down onto the ground.'
104 A more literal translation would be 'if it sits in my mind.' See page 18V and footnote 63.

Now I the master grab my partner with both hands, I can strike you with the iron both from above and from below.

I am indeed prepared to send you down onto the ground, and I will give many bad things to your head if I feel like it.

This is another motion to lay out your partner on the ground, nevertheless he who attempts to play in a similar way is not safe.

In this way, I can indeed send you down onto the ground again, from where I myself will prepare worse things for you.

32v Top

This is another motion to lay out your partner on the ground, nevertheless he who attempts to play in a similar way is not safe.

After stopping the dagger attack from above, the garter wearing student is performing another upper bind. The student's left hand has slipped behind the opponent's right wrist. He has grasped his own right wrist with his left hand. The student's left leg is leading and is to the inside of the opponent's. From here, with a sharp twist to the right, the student can throw the opponent. The Getty depicts the foot to the outside, while the Pisani-Dossi has the student's right leg leading and behind the opponent's.

From the Getty and Novati.

32v Bottom

In this way, I can indeed send you down onto the ground again, from where I myself will prepare worse things for you.

After stopping the dagger attack from above, the garter wearing student performs a throw by having his left hand slide to the opponent's elbow, while his right hand grasps their right thigh. His left hand pushes the elbow away while his right hand pulls the opponent's thigh toward him to enable the throw.

33r:

33r Top

I myself[105] will turn your dagger with a twisting in such a way because I would capture you if you should either prevent me or fight back.

After stopping the dagger attack from above, the garter wearing student performs a disarm by taking his right hand to the outside of the opponent's dagger and grasping it. He then turns the dagger toward the opponent's thumb, in a horizontal fashion, to achieve the disarm.

33r Bottom

If I now attempt to take your dagger near the elbow you indeed will see yourself suddenly stripped of that (dagger).

The garter wearing student is performing a disarm similar to the prior play. Because the dagger's point is directed at the ground and not at the student, he grips the dagger with his right hand and rotates it upwards toward the opponent's thumb.

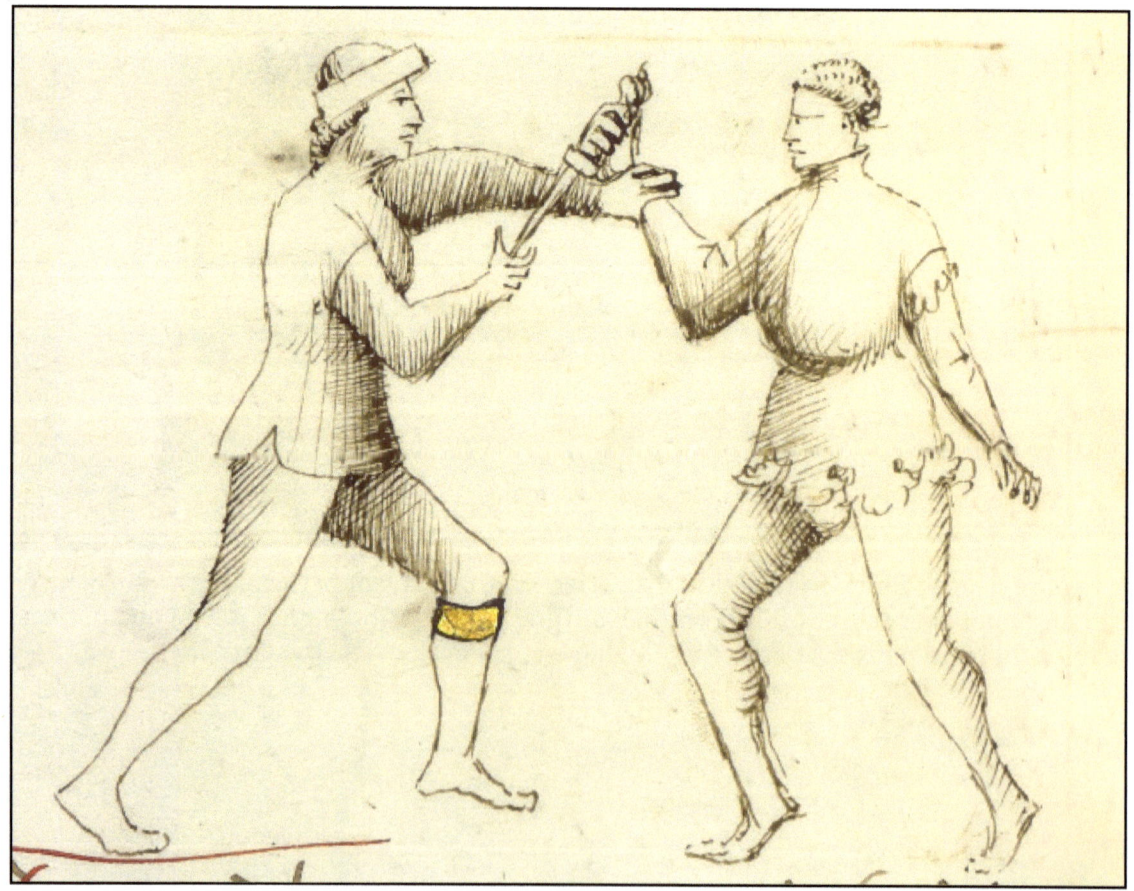

From the Getty MS Ludwig XV 13.

---

105   words 'scilicet ego' (I, of course) is written on top of the word 'ipse' (I myself). See footnote 50.

I myself will turn your dagger with a twisting in
such a way because I would capture you if you
should either prevent me or fight back.

If I now attempt to take your dagger near the elbow
you indeed will see yourself suddenly stripped of that
(dagger).

¶ I now seek this opposition with both hands in order that I may defend myself just as that master does, who captures his partner by fighting with both hands.

¶ You take me by the chest, you still might not be able to strike me, nevertheless I will tie this arm of yours in a knot by fighting.

33v Top

I now seek this opposition with both hands in order that I may defend myself just as that master does, who captures his partner[106] by fighting with both hands.

The crowned master is depicted as a crowned and garter wearing counter-master in the Getty version of the Flower of Battle. The counter-master prevents the play of 32r top by grasping his own dagger, so that his dagger is on the outside of the opponent's right hand. With a pull down and a pass back the counter-master can ruin the hands of the opponent.

The remedy master of 32r.

33v Bottom

You take me by the chest, you still might not be able to strike me, nevertheless I will tie this arm of yours in a knot by fighting.

The crowned master has been grabbed by the collar while the opponent prepares to strike. The master grips the opponent's left wrist with his left hand and pulls it close to his chest, while his right hand delivers a strike to the opponent's elbow. This must be done quickly and with extreme force to prevent the opponent from carrying out his attack.

---

106   Here the word 'sodalez' is used for partner, which is used on 26V and 36R. The word 'socius' is used for 'partner' on 22V, 31R, 32R, 32V, 43V.

34r Top

I will now strike you near your elbow, then you will release me, and I will forcefully attack your dagger straight away.

The garter wearing student is demonstrating another way to defeat the collar grab. He grips his right wrist with his left hand and turns sharply to the left to destroy the opponent's arm before he can strike.

34r Bottom

I will strike above the elbow or fist quickly, and I will miserably tie you in a in that place where you will let go of my chest.

The garter wearing student is demonstrating another way to defeat the collar grab. The student crosses his arms above his head and brings them down with all his strength. The opponent's wrist and elbow will be damaged unless he lets go.

The remedy master of 33v.

¶ I will now strike you near your elbow, then you will release me, and I will forcefully attack your dagger straight away.

¶ I will strike above the elbow or fist quickly, and I will miserably tie you in a in that place where you will let go of my chest.

¶ I attempt an action by which I will bend you back, if I do not lay you low I will perhaps prepare/attempt a better action.

¶ I am safely able to trust that you will now rush into the ground. Your dagger will really not be able to harm me.

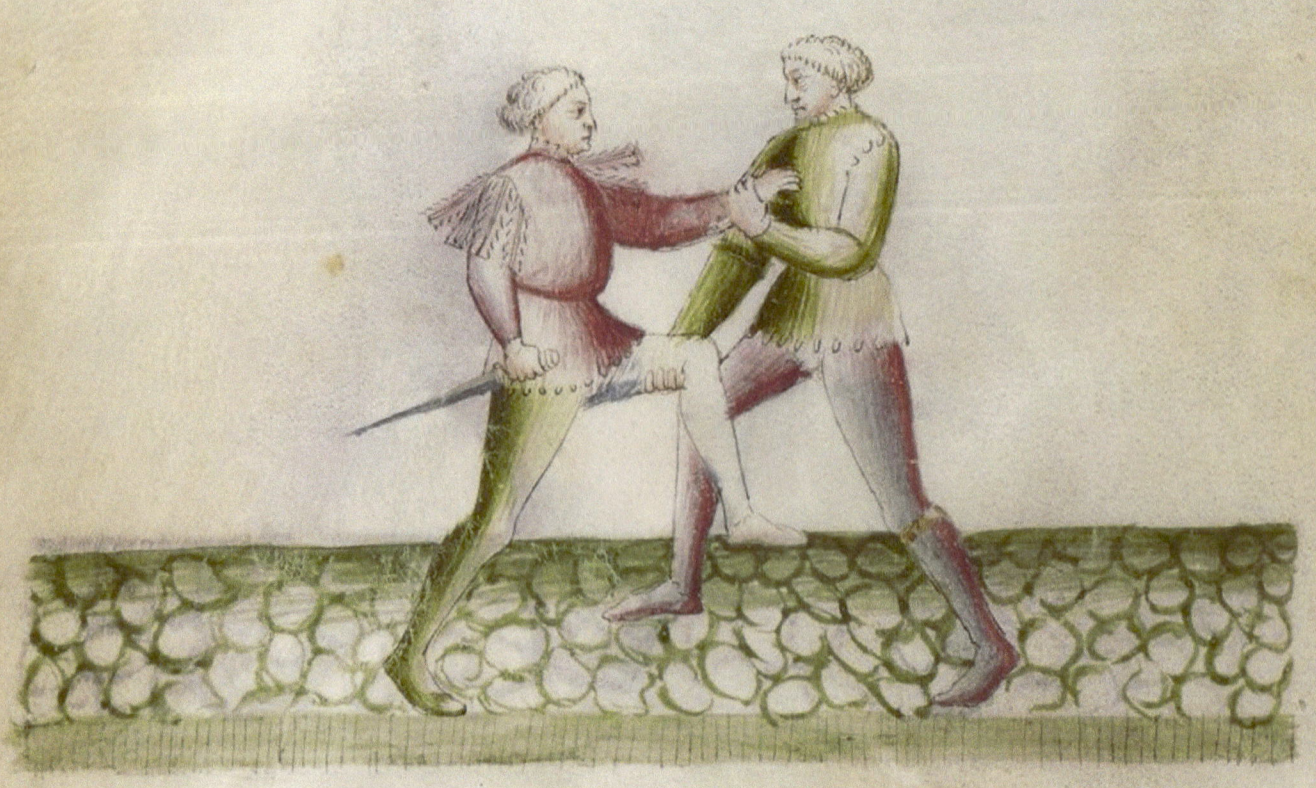

34v:

34v Top

I attempt an action by which I will bend you back, if I do not lay you low I will perhaps prepare/attempt a better action.

The garter wearing student is demonstrating another way to defeat the collar grab. The student moves his right elbow over the opponent's left, while his left hand grips the opponent's left wrist. By turning sharply to the left, the student can throw the opponent, though the Getty warns that this may not work and the technique may need to be abandoned and the opponent's dagger wielding arm sought instead.

34v Bottom

I am safely able to trust that you will now rush into the ground.[107] Your dagger will really not be able to harm me.

The garter wearing student is demonstrating another way to defeat the collar grab. He has gripped the opponent's left wrist with his left hand, while his right hand reaches under the opponent's knee. The student places their right foot behind the opponent's left foot. The Getty version also notes if the play is not successful, to seek out other ones.

The remedy master of 33v.

---

107   What is interesting is that the phrase 'that you will now rush into the ground' is written as a purpose clause instead of the more classical Latin indirect statement. This is similar to the way modern Romance languages render indirect statements.

35r Top

> *I will not have been deceived while breaking the left arm, which I hold weighed down by the right shoulder while fighting.*

The garter wearing student is demonstrating another way to defeat the collar grab. He has quickly grasped the opponent's left wrist with both hands. By turning hard to the left, the student breaks the opponent's left arm over his right shoulder. The hands of the student need to try and guide the opponent's elbow to be in such a position as to not be able to bend and thus easier to break. The Getty suggests this play is best performed in armor.

35r Bottom

> *I hold you in such a position and I grab you groaning because you are now spread with your shoulders onto the lowest ground.*

The garter wearing student is demonstrating another way to defeat the collar grab. The student has stepped deeply, placing his right leg on the inside of the opponent's left leg. His left arm has hooked under the opponent's left thigh, while his right hand has grasped the opponent's right wrist. By driving forward the student can bring the opponent to the ground.

The remedy master of 33v.

I will not have been deceived while breaking the left arm, which I hold weighed down by the right shoulder while fighting.

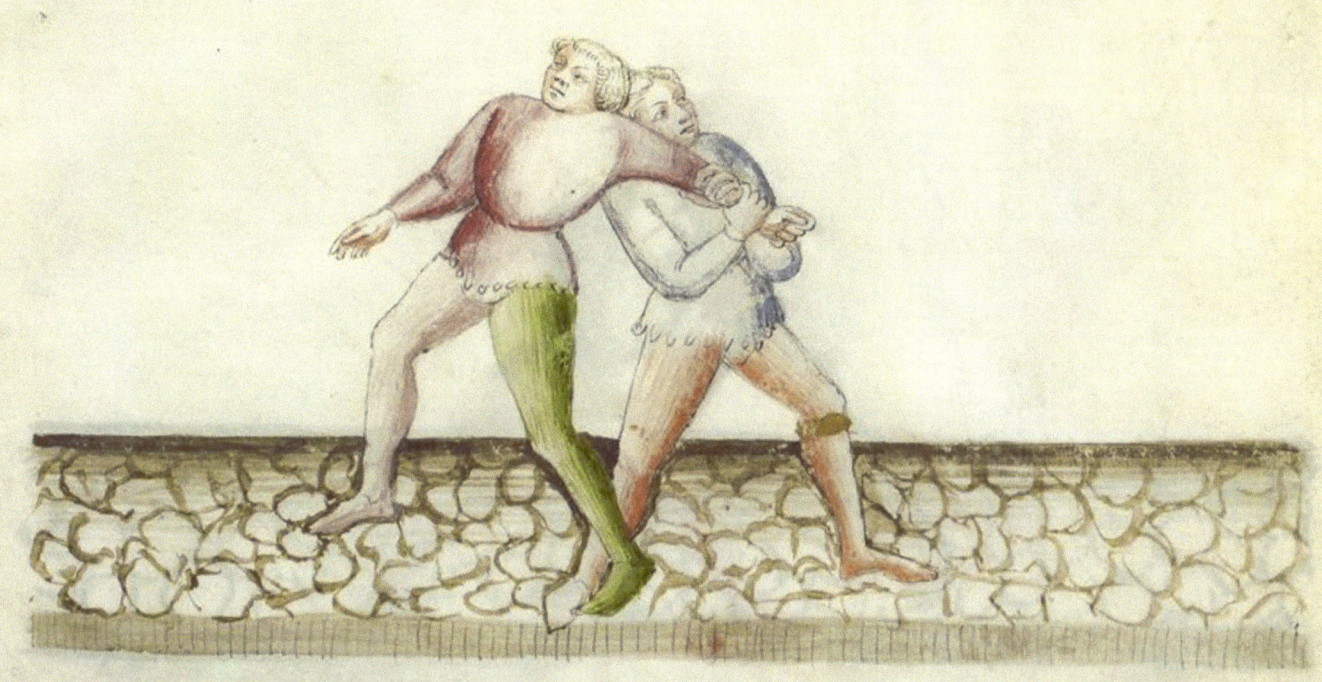

I hold you in such a position and I grab you groaning because you are now spread with your shoulders onto the lowest ground.

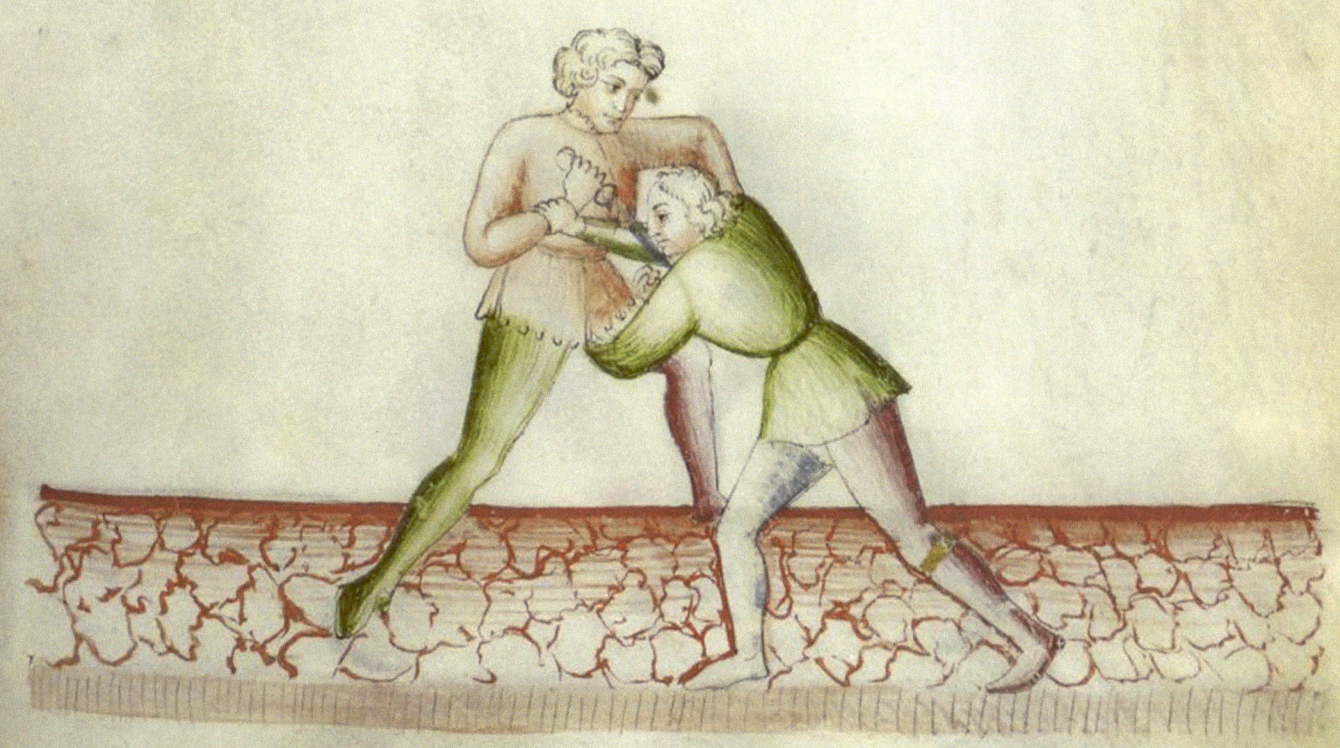

¶ Now I make this defense by means of which I may be able to take away your dagger, but I can hurt you with many plays.

¶ If I can roll you now by struggling against your arm I will quickly make you dip in a lower key.

35v Top

Now I make this defense by means of which[108] I may be able to take away your dagger, but I can hurt you with many plays.

The garter wearing student is demonstrating another way to defeat the collar grab. The student has passed deeply forward with his left leg while his arms have crossed and driven under the opponent's dagger strike. The two crossed arms can prevent even a powerful blow. From here, various locks, binds and throws can be sought.

35v Bottom

If I can roll you now by struggling against your arm I will quickly make you dip in a lower key.

The garter wearing student is demonstrating another way to defeat the collar grab. The student's right hand has gone under the opponent's left arm and gripped their triceps. The student then passes forward and turns sharply to the left to try and put the opponent into the lower lock. The Getty suggests this play be performed in armor.

The remedy master of 33v.

---

108   The word 'quo' should probably be qua since its antecedent, 'tecturam' is a feminine noun. Berthaut points out that the words 'pro ut' (as, just as), is written above 'quo' (by means of which).

36r Top

>Because I now hold you while fighting with both hands,[109] I will snatch away your dagger just as you certainly deserve.

The garter wearing student is demonstrating another way to defeat the collar grab. The student grips the opponent's right wrist with his left hand, and the opponent's right elbow with his right hand. The two hands prevent the opponent from striking and allow the following play.

The remedy master of 33v.

36r Bottom

>Now I teach you to take away a dagger while struggling with your partner,[110] this is because the student did not know to fight first.

From the prior play, the student has passed in. His left hand remains gripped, but the right has grasped the dagger to seek a disarm. To complete the disarm the student pushes the dagger down and to the right toward the thumb of the opponent where his grip is the weakest.

---

109   Here the phrase 'gemellis manibus' is used to mean 'both hands' instead of 'palmis binis,' which was used in 33V. 'Gemellis manibus' is also used on 42V.

110   Here the word 'sodali' is used for 'partner,' just like 26V, and 33V. The word 'socius' is used for 'partner' on 22V, 31R, 32R, 32V, 43V.

Because I now hold you while fighting with both hands, I will snatch away your dagger just as you certainly deserve.

Now I teach you to take away a dagger while struggling with your partner, this is because the student did not know to fight first.

¶ I do not know a man with whom I would not be able to fight if we both lead by turning dagger into dagger whether I should be armed or if I should perhaps be lacking arms, and this movement would be pleasing so long as this play has been carried out exactly.

¶ I perform this guard when I have been protected in armor, and suddenly into the middle key which ends all war, and nobody is effective when they attempt an attack against it, I will enter, nobody fighting back was able to oppose me.

36v:

36v Top

I do not know a man with whom I would not be able to fight if we both lead by turning dagger into dagger whether I should be armed or if I should perhaps be lacking arms,[111] and this movement would be pleasing so long as this play has been carried out exactly.

The crowned master has a dagger of his own and prevents an attack by grabbing his own dagger and bringing his hands upwards. The two hands defeat the one of the opponent.

36v Bottom

I perform this guard when I have been protected in armor, and suddenly into the middle key which ends all war, and nobody is effective when they attempt an attack against it,[112] I will enter, nobody fighting back was able to oppose me.

The crowned master has a dagger of his own and is holding it with crossed arms. As before, the opponent's attack is defeated by bringing his hands upwards. The two hands defeat the one of the opponent. From here the middle lock can be sought.

From the Getty and the middle lock of 24r.

---

111   A more literal translation would be 'when arms are lacking.'
112   A more literal translation would be 'when they drag warlike things against it.'

37r Top

I carry my dagger in this cross while fighting, no defense of the giving dagger stands in its way in the play, but I will be able to destroy you with many motions in the play.

The crowned master has defeated a thrust from below by holding his dagger with both hands. The dagger is brought down and the student's two hands defeat the opponent's one. From here the lower lock can be sought.

The lower lock of 31v.

37r Bottom

This motion is indeed superior to someone holding their dagger in a cross, for it certainly was able to work in armor both above and below, this lower play rushes openly to the lower bind, the middle bind perhaps lies under at the end.

The crowned master has a dagger of his own and is holding it with crossed arms. He has defeated a low thrust by bringing his dagger to the left where his two hands defeat the opponent's one.

¶I carry my dagger in this cross while fighting, no defense of the giving dagger stands in its way in the play, but I will be able to destroy you with many motions in the play.

¶This motion is indeed superior to someone holding their dagger in a cross, for it certainly was able to work in armor both above and below, this lower play rushes openly to the lower bind, the middle bind perhaps lies under at the end.

¶ The student will be able to make this play of that master, and to take away the powerful dagger.

¶ Behold! I have crossed under the arm in the play, I have even left the disarm but I will bind your back.

37v

37v Top

The student will be able to make this play of that master, and to take away the powerful dagger.

The depiction is of a counter-master with a crown and garter. In the Getty he is shown as a master, preventing a low thrust. This prevention is seen in 38r bottom. The follow up student's left hand grips the opponent's right wrist, and his left hand grips slightly above. A disarm is then performed with the right hand, by gripping the opponent's dagger and turning it towards his thumb. The Paris shows the mislabeled counter-master driving the opponent's own dagger into their chest.

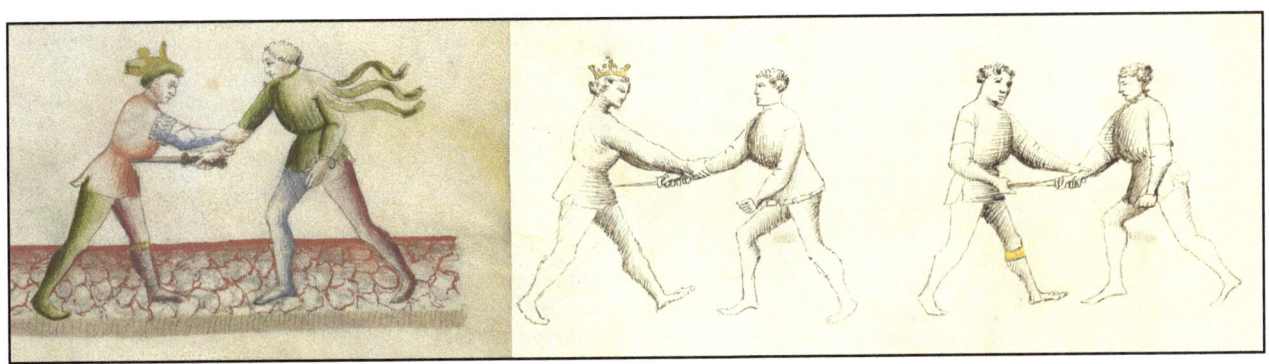

38r and the master and following play from the Getty.

37v Bottom

Behold! I have crossed under the arm in the play, I have even left the disarm but I will bind your back.

The garter wearing student has prevented a low thrust with both hands as seen in 38r bottom. From here, he has turned sharply to the right and is breaking the opponent's arm over his left shoulder.

38r:

38r Top

I prepare to take your life with a lower bind, if perhaps I am able to turn your arm.

The Paris depicts the student with a crown, but in the Getty he is not a counter-master. After preventing a low thrust as seen in the following play, the student pushes the opponent's blade to his left. This allows him to release his left hand and seek a lower lock.

The lower lock of 31v.

38r Bottom

I am indeed able to tie down your arm in a similar way as it is binding together from a lower key.

As before, there is an artistic error in the depiction of a student. The person depicted is either a master preventing a thrust from below, or, he is a student who has pushed the low attack to his right. From here he can try to break the opponent's elbow or seek a lower lock.

¶ I prepare to take your life with a lower bind, if perhaps
I am able to turn your arm.

¶ I am indeed able to tie down your arm in a similar
way as it is binding together from a lower key.

¶ I indeed was prepared in order that I may gain holds for myself, if I do not deceive you I will be able to benefit for a short time.

¶ I seek to change the way by which I am able to deceive you, here I will turn you to the ground by means of your rushing chest.

¶ If you do not conquer by your skill, which I can believe, you yourself will suffer many very bad things from my strength.

¶ Behold, I come with arms held to conquer lustful intentions, in order that I may gain strong holds for myself in the play.

38v Top

I indeed was prepared in order that I may gain holds for myself, if I do not deceive you I will be able to benefit for a short time.

I seek to change the way by which I am able to deceive you, here I will turn you to the ground by means of your rushing chest.

The crowned master on the left is in the Long guard. The guard is used to prevent the customary grapples an opponent will seek and follow up with a break to the arm. The master's right arm is extended further in the Getty than depicted in the Paris.

The crowned master on the right is in the Boar's Tooth guard which can counter the grapple attempted by moving into the guard of the Iron Gate.

38v Bottom

If you do not conquer by your skill, which I can believe, you yourself[113] will suffer many very bad things from my strength.

Behold, I come with arms held to conquer lustful intentions,[114] in order that I may gain strong holds for myself in the play.

The crowned master on the left is in the guard of Iron Gate. The Getty indicates from this guard the master can seek grapples and binds, not only in wrestling, but also with the dagger, sword, spear and poleaxe as well.

The crowned master on the right is in the Front guard. The master can approach his opponents and seek to grip them, and then from there move into Iron Gate to throw the opponent, or to seek a variety of locks and holds.

---

113   'Scilicet tu' (certainly you) is written above 'ipse' (you yourself). See footnote 50.
114   The phrase 'lustful intentions' humorously refers to the fact that the opponent is attempting the same sort of embrace that one would give to a lover.

39r:

39r Top

With this hold I will make you touch the ground, or maybe I will tie your left arm in knots.

The crowned master has either prevented his opponent from coming to grips and seeking a grip similar to that of 41r bottom, or he has approached in the Front guard and sought this grapple. The left hand jams the opponent's right arm in the elbow preventing it from moving. The right arm has allowed the opponent's left hand to grip the master's back. The master's right arm is pushing upwards from the outside to try and turn the opponent's arm.

The play of 41r. This grip is being prevented.

39r Bottom

I will force you to lick the dirty ground with your face, or I will make miserable you enter under the lowest key.

This follow up play depicts a master, but in the other treatises is shown as a student and is likely an error on the artist's part, or a decision to follow the instructions of the Getty manuscript, which says the prior play and this one are joined. The depicted master is carrying on from the prior master, fully turning the opponent's left arm so as to straighten the elbow. His left hand has gripped his own right wrist. The master's right leg has crossed in front of his left, so that he can sharply turn to the left. This will uncross his legs and provide the power needed to break the opponent's arm which is locked in place over the master's shoulder.

¶ With this hold I will make you touch the ground, or maybe I will tie your left arm in knots.

¶ I will force you to lick the dirty ground with your face, or I will make miserable you enter under the lowest key.

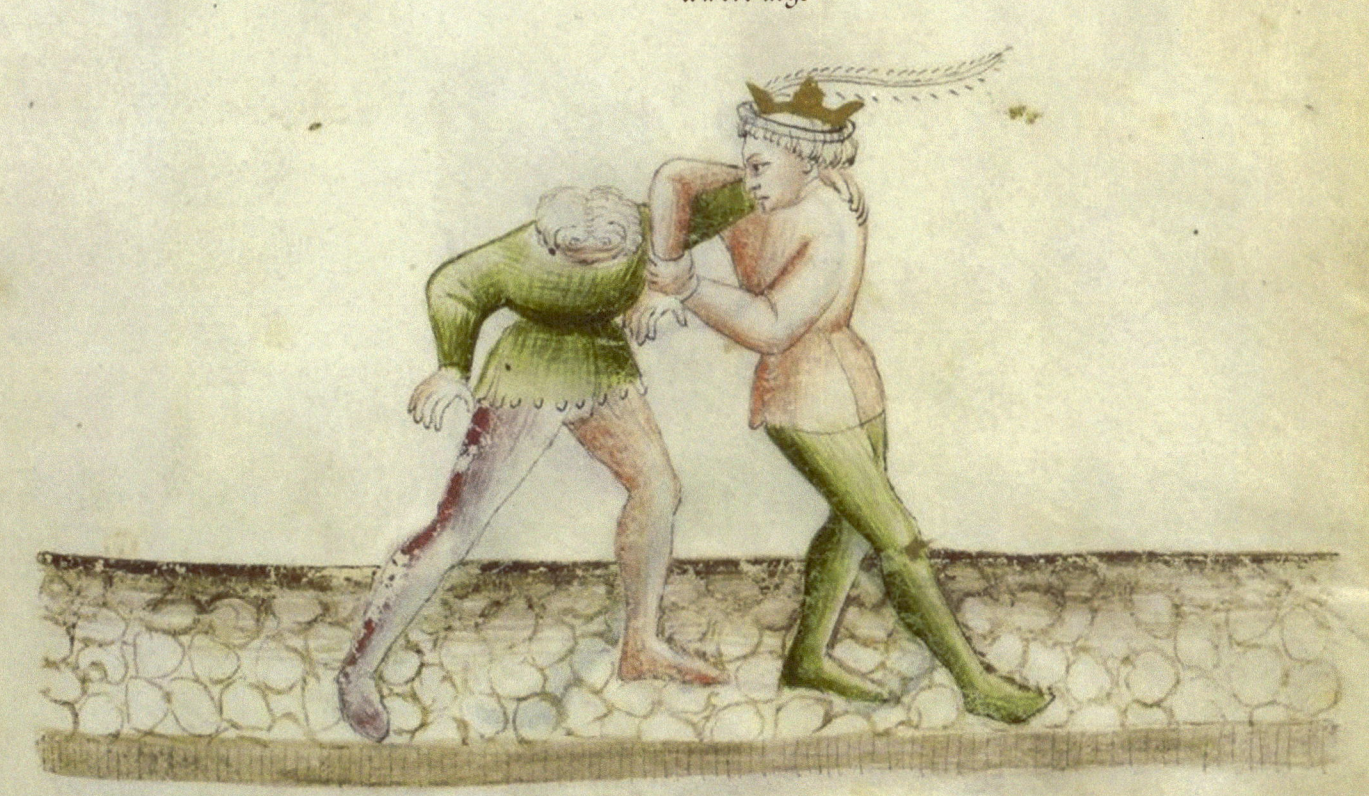

❧ I will throw you straight away onto the lowest ground from your kidneys, you will not be able to get up without grievous punishment.

❧ I would be making you fall on the ground with a hold if you were better in the play than all the masters.

39v Top

I will throw you straight away onto the lowest ground from your kidneys, you will not be able to get up without grievous punishment.

This play follows from the prior master of 39r top. If the opponent retracts their left arm to prevent the break, the garter wearing student moves into this position. The right hand pushes the opponent's jaw and the left hand grabs under the opponent's knee. The student's right leg is behind the opponent's left. From here he can throw his opponent who has to contend with a pull against his neck and jaw, the lifting of his leg and the student's leg up against him. Even a larger opponent will have a hard time preventing this because where the head is pulled, so too will the body try to follow.

The remedy master of 39r.

39v Bottom

I would be making you fall on the ground with a hold if you were better in the play than all the masters.

The crowned and garter wearing counter-master is shown as a student in other versions of the Flower of Battle and the instructions from the other treatises do not indicate this to be a counter-master, but rather a student. The depicted counter-master is performing a play similar to the one prior. In this variation, the opponent is seeking a grapple as seen in 41r bottom. To prevent this grapple the depicted counter-master has placed his right hand upon the jaw of the opponent and the left hand is placed against the opponent's right arm. By pulling everything to the right, the depicted counter-master can throw his opponent over his right leg and to the ground.

The play of 41r. This grip is being prevented.

40r:

40r Top

You will smash the ground from the top because of the hold by which I wrestle above[115] and below, the fates will not deny.

The crowned and garter wearing counter-master is shown as a student in other versions of the Flower of Battle and as before the instructions from the other treatises do not indicate this to be a counter-master. The opponent has successfully wrapped his arms around the waist of his opponent. The depicted counter-master in response has his right foot behind the opponent's left. His right arm grips the opponent by the jaw and is pulling up and to the right, following the concept that where the head goes, the body follows. The depicted counter-master's left hand is gripped to the opponent's waist. By pulling everything to the right, the depicted counter-master can throw his opponent over his right leg and to the ground.

40r Bottom

I have placed my palms on your face, but nevertheless I moved them freely from there, to where I can overwhelm you with other holds, which I now attempt to show.

The crowned and garter wearing counter-master is preventing the prior technique. Before being thrown, the counter-master uses his right hand to push the opponent's elbow upwards and to the left. This turns the opponent and at the same time causes him to lose his grip on the counter-master's jaw. From here, the opponent can be thrown leftwards over the counter-master's leg, or other locks and grips can be sought.

---

115   In the phrase 'Propter prensuram supra qua luctor' the word 'qua' (by which) has the letter 'a' annotated on top of it and the word 'supra' (above) has the letter 'b' written on top to show the order of translation (Berthaut). This is one of three times (the others are 41R and 43R) this annotation appears in the manual. This is probably text's owner's annotation added to facilitate his reading.

¶ You will smash the ground from the top because of the hold by which I wrestle above and below, the fates will not deny.

¶ I have placed my palms on your face, but nevertheless I moved them freely from there, to where I can overwhelm you with other holds, which I now attempt to show.

¶ You will stretch onto the ground confused with sad honor, this is because I myself hold your head under the left arm.

¶ I hold my finger under this left ear in the play in order that you may lose the hold by which you were trying to overcome me.

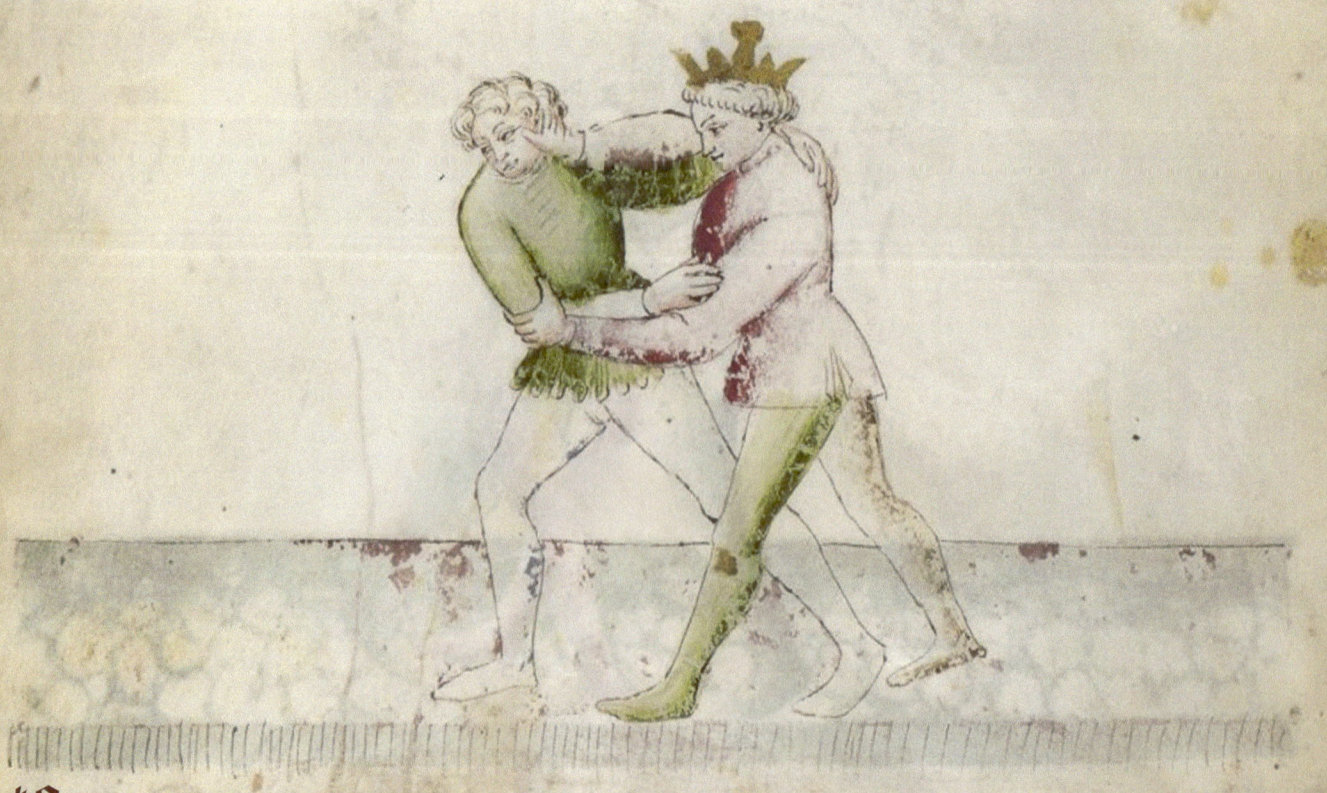

40v:

40v Top

You will stretch onto the ground confused with sad honor, this is because I myself[116] hold your head under the left arm.

The garter wearing student has placed his head under the right arm of his opponent. From here, his left hand holds to the opponent's right wrist, and his left arm scoops between the opponent's leg. The opponent can then be rotated left, up and over the shoulders of the student who can send the opponent to the ground head first. This play is similar to a fireman's carry, except the victim is not rescued, but rather thrown to the ground.

40v Bottom

I hold my finger under this left ear in the play in order that you may lose the hold by which you were trying to overcome me.

The crowned master is depicted as a student in the other versions of the Flower of Battle. To break a hold, he is driving his right thumb under the opponent's ear. To best find this pressure-point, the thumb should be bent, so the tip of the thumb is driving inwards. There is a nerve that runs along the jaw and ear. Pressing hard against this nerve causes pain. The counter to this technique is for the opponent to push under the attacker's right elbow.

---

116 'Scilicet ego' (certainly I) is written above 'ipse' (I myself). See footnote 50.

41r Top

If you[117] have also treacherously grabbed me from behind with your art, this hold will nevertheless put you onto the lowest ground.

The garter wearing student is preventing a grapple from behind. This play must be done quickly to succeed. The student has stepped backwards so that his right leg is behind his opponent's leg. By turning sharply to the right he can throw the opponent to the ground as their own grapple is used against them.

41r Bottom

Meanwhile this play of turning the legs[118] is praised, nevertheless it is not suitable for it often deceives those who attempt it.

The garter wearing student and his opponent have come into a traditional grapple. Neither has advantage and both can throw the other over their lead legs. In the other versions of the Flower of Battle the technique is warned against because it must be done quickly and often fails. However, it is clearly a common hold and is often what the opponents are trying to accomplish against the student. This may be the reason for showing it.

---

117   'Si tu' (if you) is written above 'proditor' (treacherously) (Berthaut).

118   Four words in the phrase 'ludus hic interdum celebrator crura rotandi' (Meanwhile this play of twisting the legs) have the letters a, b, c, and d written on top of them to show the order of translation (Berthaut). This is one of three times (the others are on 40R and 43R) this annotation appears in the manual. This is probably text's owner's annotation added to facilitate his reading.

If you have also treacherously grabbed me from behind with your art, this hold will nevertheless put you onto the lowest ground.

Meanwhile this play of turning the legs is praised, nevertheless it is not suitable for it often deceives those who attempt it.

¶ When this hold is understood by an agreeing mind it is called external, with this I will finally make you continue sadly.

¶ I myself will shatter your testicles in such a way with a hard knee because there will be no strength in your heart.

41v Top

When this hold is understood by an agreeing mind it is called external, with this I will finally make you continue sadly.

The garter wearing student has grappled the opponent from behind before they could attempt the play in 41r top. The opponent has few options at this point and can be held or thrown to the ground. In the Getty version of the Flower of Battle Fiore says the only counter is to run backwards toward a wall or post and hope crashing into it will force the opponent to release his grip.

41v Bottom

I myself[119] will shatter your testicles in such a way with a hard knee because there will be no strength in your heart.[120]

The garter wearing student and opponent entered into similar grips, with each grabbing the other around the waist. The student has driven his knee upwards into the groin of his opponent. From here, the student can more easily attempt a throw. A counter to this is for the opponent to try and grip beneath the knee before the student can complete the strike. Understandably, such a counter must be done quickly.

---

119   'Scilicet ego' (certainly I) is written above 'ipse' (I myself). See footnote 50.
120   Berthaut notes that the perfect subjunctive verb 'aderint' is used instead of the future indicative verb 'aderunt' because the subjunctive mood is usually used in subordinate clauses, such as the one introduced by 'quod' (because).

42r:

42r Top

As many times as you will quickly abandon me while I am playing with you, by that number I multiply the pains in your suffering nose, I trust.[121]

The garter wearing student has been gripped around the waist. To break the hold he has driven his hands, one over the other, into the face of the opponent trying to break their nose and push back the head. As before, where the head goes the body follows and the opponent's grip can be broken.

42r Bottom

With a similar hold I have, as we say, brought down your limbs. Nevertheless, you yourself[122] *will miserably go away in the opposite direction because you are about to fall, as you duly see if you perceive it in the light.*

The garter wearing student is shown as a counter-master in the Getty and Pisani-Dossi manuscripts. This play prevents the prior one. The counter-master has driven his right hand under the left wrist or elbow of the opponent. The left hand is gripping the opponent's left leg under the knee and pulls upwards to assist in a throw.

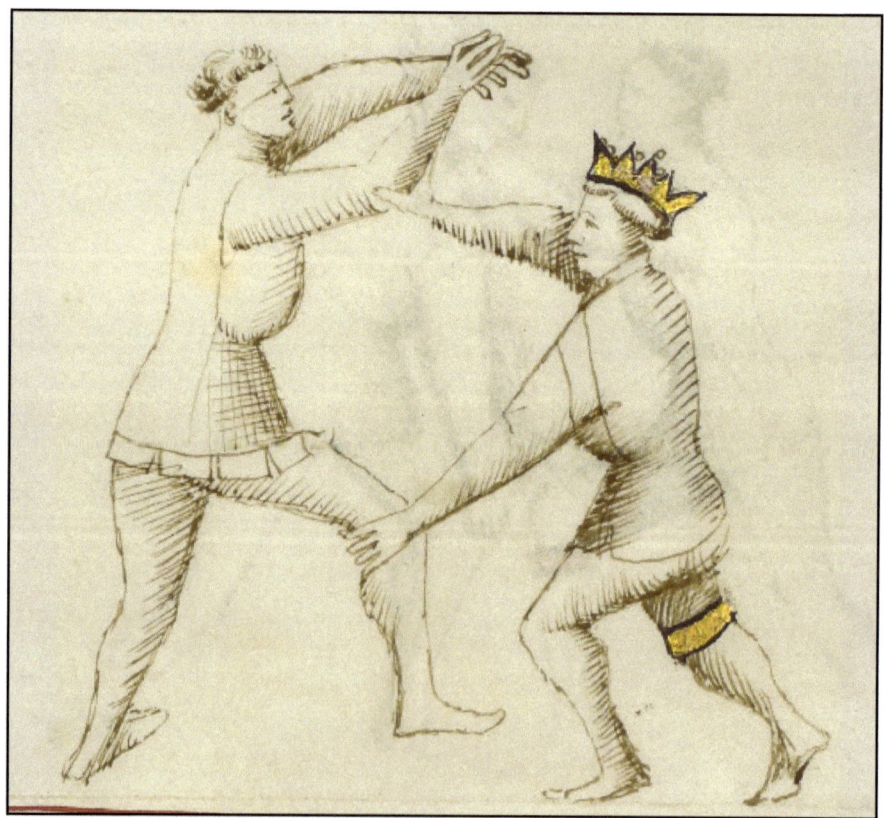

From the Getty MS Ludwig XV 13.

---

121 I had to take some liberties with the Latin in order to make this passage understandable in English.
122 'tu scilicet' (certainly you) is once again above 'ipse' (you yourself). See footnote 50.

As many times as you will quickly abandon me while I am playing with you, by that number I multiply the pains in your suffering nose, I trust.

With a similar hold I have, as we say, brought down your limbs. Nevertheless, you yourself will miserably go away in the opposite direction because you are about to fall, as you duly see if you perceive it in the light.

And under your chin I bring you more pains, in order that I may touch the lowest ground with your sad kidneys.

By playing the face with both hands in front here, this counter will also hurt the eye more from there.

42v Top

And under your chin I bring you more pains, in order that I may touch the lowest ground with your sad kidneys.

The garter wearing student is performing a play similar to that of 42r top. In this case, the opponent has grappled around the neck of the student instead of the waist. The student's arms have moved to the outside of the opponent's arms, and his joined hands are pushing hard and up into the opponent's jaw. The opponent's head will be forced back so as to break the opponent's hold.

The play of 42r.

42v Bottom

By playing the face with both hands[123] in front here, this counter will also hurt the eye more from there.

The garter wearing student is shown as a counter-master in other versions of the Flower of Battle. This play counters the prior one. The counter-master, realizing his head is being pushed back has brought his thumbs to the eyes of the opponent. Because his opponent's arms are to the outside of his, he can bring his elbows over the opponent's and force them down. The gouging of the eyes and use of the elbows breaks the opponent's hold.

---

123 Just like on 36R, the phrase 'gemellis manibus' is used for 'both hands.' On 33V, the phrase 'binis palmis' is used to mean 'both hands.'

43r Top

> *It is permitted that this play is scarcely known in this art,[124] nevertheless the play itself[125] really comes from an experienced man.*

The garter wearing student is performing an unusual play after preventing a low thrust as seen in 38r bottom. The opponent, finding their thrust prevented has pushed downwards to free their dagger. The student pressed down as well, and his left hand reached behind and around the opponent's leg to grip their right wrist. From here he has passed behind the opponent and brought his right hand to disarm the opponent's dagger.

The play from 38r.

43r Bottom

> *I really protect the opposite of the first master, and with this covering I will now show very many bad things.*

The garter wearing and crowned counter-master is defeating the play from 21v top. As the opponent reaches their left hand up to grab, the counter-master has brought his left hand up. The opponent has grasped the wrong hand, allowing the counter-master to strike his opponent.

The remedy master of 21v.

---

124   Just like on 40R and 41R, the letters 'a,' 'b,' and 'c' are written on top of three words in the phrase 'iste licet ludus vix sit hac cognitus arte' (It is permitted that this play is scarcely known in this art). Similar to 40R and 41R, the letters appear to indicate the order of translation and were probably added by the text's owner to facilitate reading.

125   For once, ipse is used without 'ego/tu scilicet.' Perhaps because this time it is used in the third person (it itself) instead of the first person (I myself) or second person (you yourself).

It is permitted that this play is scarcely known in this art, nevertheless the play itself really comes from an experienced man.

I really protect the opposite of the first master, and with this covering I will now show very many bad things.

¶ I openly do the opposite of the first king as he holds back the dagger. This opens the arm to striking.

¶ Opposite of this thing which threatens very many bad things, here I govern myself in order that I may injure my partner with a lethal wound.

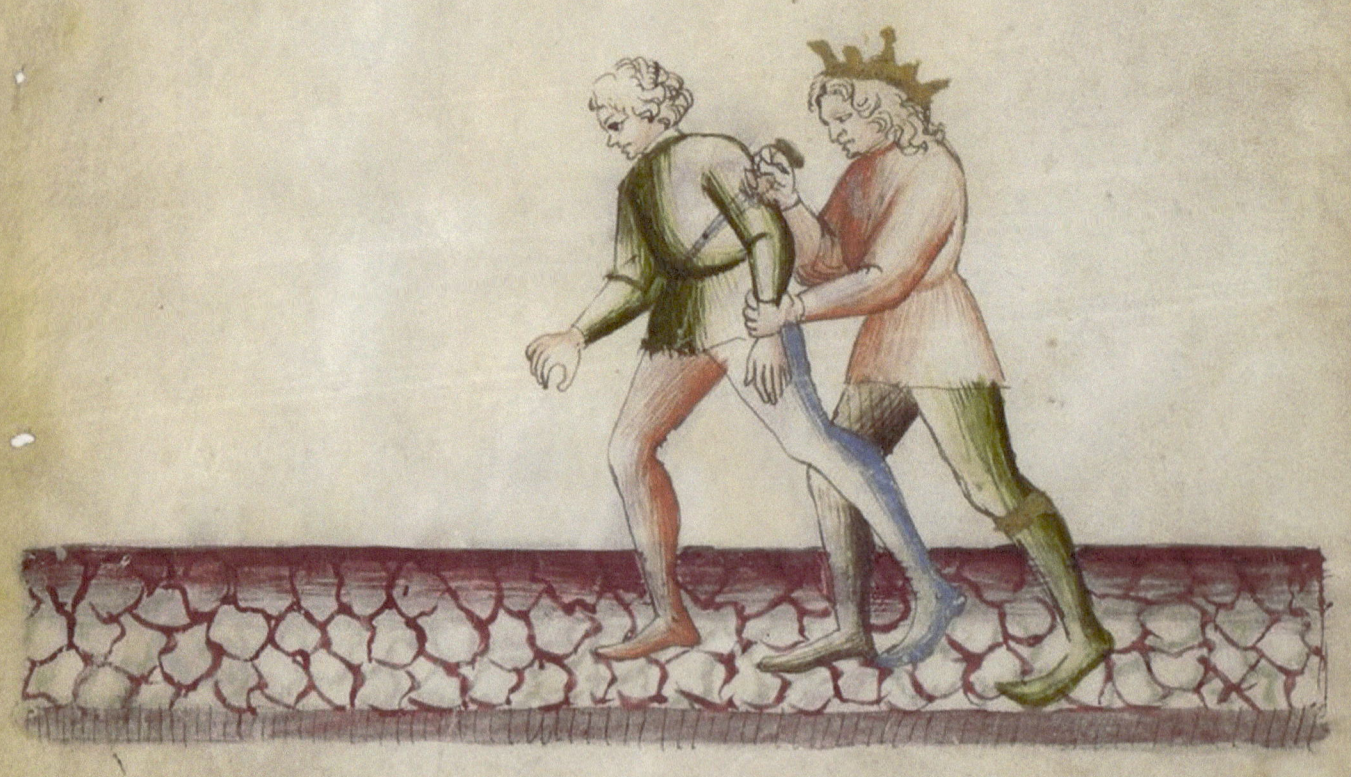

43v:

43v top

I openly do the opposite of the first king as he holds back the dagger. This opens the arm to striking.

This play is similar to one from the Pisani Dossi and is a counter to 21v top. The opponent has tried to intercept an incoming attack, and perhaps too soon, has raised his arm. The garter wearing counter-master drives his blade into the offered target.

The same play from the Pisani Dossi

43v bottom

Opposite of this thing which threatens very many bad things, here I govern myself in order that I may injure my partner[126] with a lethal wound.

This play is a follow up from 43r bottom or 44r top. Once the opponent's defense has been stopped, using either play, the left hand of the counter-master grips the opponent's wrist and pulls down, while the right hand stabs with the dagger into the opponent's chest or back.

The counters from 43r bottom and 44r top.

---

126   Here the word 'sociuz' is used for partner, just like on 22V, 31R, 32R, and 32V. The word 'sodalis' is used on 26V, 33V, 36R.

44r:

44r top

It is neither work nor is it punishment for me while performing a tenacious bind by means of which I will now be able to injure you and I will strike your kidneys powerfully with a large wound.

The crowned and garter wearing counter-master is thwarting the opponent's defense from 21v by grabbing his own dagger and trapping the opponent's wrist in a vice. A sharp pull to the left brings the opponent down and exposes their back. From here, the prior play from 43v bottom can be performed.

Florius, a most experienced author, once brought forth this book, therefore the greatest honor of praise must truly be given to him, a man from the Furlana family.

It is neither work nor is it punishment for me while performing a tenacious bind by means of which I will now be able to injure you and I will strike your kidneys powerfully with a large wound.

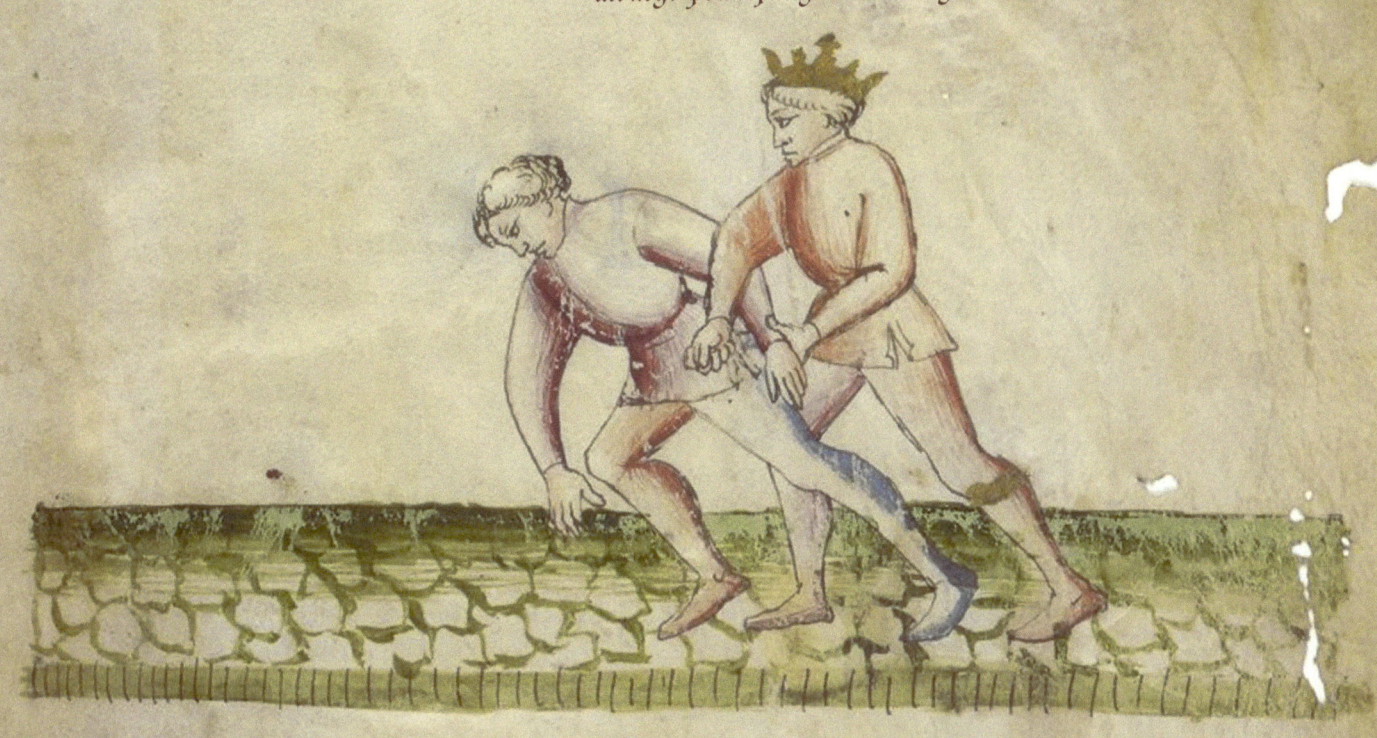

Florius, a most experienced author, once brought forth this book, therefore the greatest honor of praise must truly be given to him, a man from the Furlana family.

Bibliography

Fiore de'i Liberi, *Florius de Arte Luctandi*. Edited and Translated into French by Charlélie Berthaut. (April, 2013), http://www.ilcerchiodiferro.it/trattati/florius-de-arte-luctandi-ms-latin-11269.pdf

Wiktenauer. "Florius de Arte Luctandi (MS Latin 11269)." Last modified December 21, 2016. http://wiktenauer.com/wiki/Florius_de_Arte_Luctandi_(MS_Latin_11269).

Wiktenauer. "Fiore de'i Liberi." Last modified September 27, 2016. http://wiktenauer.com/wiki/Fiore_de%27i_Liberi.

Wiktenauer. "Fior di Battaglia (MS Ludwig XV 13)." Last modified October 19, 2016. http://wiktenauer.com/wiki/Fior_di_Battaglia_(MS_Ludwig_XV_13).

Wiktenauer. "Flos Duellatorum (Pisani Dossi MS)." Last modified October 19, 2016. http://wiktenauer.com/wiki/Flos_Duellatorum_(Pisani_Dossi_MS).

Wiktenauer. "Fior di Battaglia (MS M.383)." Last modified February 19, 2017. http://wiktenauer.com/wiki/Fior_di_Battaglia_(MS_M.383).

www.ingramcontent.com/pod-product-compliance
Lightning Source LLC
Chambersburg PA
CBHW041543220426
43665CB00002B/20